SIDREA Series in Accounting and Business Administration

This is the official book series of SIDREA - the Italian Society of Accounting and Business Administration. This book series is provided with a wide Scientific Committee composed of Academics by SIDREA. It publishes contributions (monographs, edited volumes and proceedings) as a result of the double blind review process by the SIDREA's thematic research groups, operating at the national and international levels. Particularly, the series aims to disseminate specialized findings on several topics – classical and cutting-edge alike – that are currently being discussed by the accounting and business administration communities. The series authors are respected researchers and professors in the fields of business valuation; governance and internal control; financial accounting; public accounting; management control; gender; turnaround predictive models; non-financial disclosure; intellectual capital, smart technologies, and digitalization; and university governance and performance measurement. This book series is indexed in Scopus.

Mohamed Aman • Lorenzo Lucianetti

Corporate Environmental Performance and Environmental Management Accounting Systems

Springer

Mohamed Aman
University of Chieti-Pescara
Pescara, Italy

Lorenzo Lucianetti
University of Chieti-Pescara
Pescara, Italy

ISSN 2662-9879 ISSN 2662-9887 (electronic)
SIDREA Series in Accounting and Business Administration
ISBN 978-3-031-84949-7 ISBN 978-3-031-84947-3 (eBook)
https://doi.org/10.1007/978-3-031-84947-3

This Springer imprint is published by the registered company Springer Nature Switzerland AG
The registered company address is: Gewerbestrasse 11, 6330 Cham, Switzerland

Preface

Controversial environmental issues are highly challenged topics in the business world. In recent years, customers and other stakeholders have become more concerned with an organization's accomplishments regarding overall performance, not merely making progress in an organizational context. They evaluate the organization's contribution to building a sustainable society. In order to handle carbon emissions and climate change, critical undertakings such as environmental preservation and environmentally aware actions are an integral part of the overall strategy. Environmental management accounting (EMA) is, therefore, essential in creating a situation in which the organization handles various environmental problems proactively. To that end, the organization has developed environmental hazard and opportunity assessment techniques. These functions are used to scan the external and internal environments for threats to the environment and to intervene to respond to any conditions that may be problematic. EMA attempts to incorporate conventional management accounting perspectives within the environmental context. EMA provides a set of elements that can be the cornerstone for management to achieve the paramount goal of sustainable development.

Based on organizational-level data of Italian listed firms, this work explores the role played by environmental management accounting practices, the effect of distinct aspects of governance dedicated to the environment in improving corporate environmental performance, and the extent of environmental disclosure. After the introductory chapter, specifically in the second chapter, we outline the conceptualization and evolution of corporate environmental performance. Then, we discuss the measurements of corporate environmental performance and apprehend the effect on the disclosure practices in the literature. Moreover, we emphasize the purpose and implication of environmental performance measurement systems. Afterward, we highlight the overlaps between environmental accounting and corporate accountability. In Chap. 3, we described the concept of environmental management accounting, outlining the evolution of EMA, the main tools, and the consequences of adoption as an innovative tool for the organization to keep pace with the demand for environmental protection worldwide. Understanding the consequences of these tools would be essential for the organization's successful implementation of the EMA in managing its environmental matters.

In Chap. 4 (*The relationship between environmental management accounting, environmental disclosure, governance, and corporate environmental performance: Some empirical evidence from Italy*), we examine the mediating and moderating effect of EMA on the association between environmental governance and environmental performance. To this aim, we sampled 70 FTSE (100) firms listed on the Italian Stock Exchange from 2017 to 2021, considering the implementation of the Italian Legislative Decree 254/2016. The study period has witnessed unprecedented challenges to the global economy and the increasing tendency toward environmental regulations and sustainability initiatives. Drawing on the natural resource-based view and stakeholder theory, we provide the following findings. First, we evidence a positive and significant association between environmental governance and corporate environmental performance. Second, we show that environmental management accounting positively and significantly moderates and fully mediates the relationship between environmental governance and corporate environmental performance. The results confirm the potential moderating role of environmental management accounting, showing greater accountability and overseeing stakeholders' perceptions in improving the underlying relationship between environmental governance and corporate environmental performance. In addition, this study enriches the debate over the costs and benefits of environmental management system implementation, such as environmental management accounting in providing information on environmental costs, which are helpful for the management in monitoring firms' financial and environmental performance. Our findings have important implications for environmentalists, policy-makers, and regulators. Indeed, these findings may guide boards in various decision settings to minimize environmental risk and imply environmental protection practices toward the green expanse.

Pescara, Italy

Mohamed Aman
Lorenzo Lucianetti

Contents

Chapter 1
Introduction

The degradation of the environment presents a significant challenge for global development and sustainability. This underscores the importance of integrating environmental concerns into companies' business processes (Marrucci et al., 2022). Consequently, industrial firms face various pressures from stakeholders to adopt proactive environmental strategies and measures aimed at minimizing the adverse impact of their operations on the natural environment (Wang et al., 2018). Specifically, there is an increasing expectation for firms to fulfill their responsibilities and promptly address environmental issues by implementing environmental practices, initiatives, and actions to enhance their environmental performance (Lisi, 2015).

Existing research shows that the relationship between environmental governance and environmental performance is considerably complex and may be influenced by multiple factors (e.g., Albitar et al., 2023; Bui et al., 2020; Haque, 2017; Qiu et al., 2016). Thus, in order to thoroughly understand the relationship between environmental governance and environmental performance, it is imperative to extend the analysis and pinpoint the environmental factors that can mediate and/or moderate these nexus. The relationship between environmental governance and environmental performance may be affected by the advancement and application of an appropriate management accounting system. As such, environmental management accounting (hereinafter referred to as EMA) is an important communication channel of environmental performance information through which firms can manage their corporate reputation and demonstrate their accountability and transparency to stakeholders (Latan et al., 2018). Nevertheless, there is a limited understanding of how the combination of EMA systems and voluntary adoption of environmental governance measures can improve a firm's environmental performance as a whole. In this regard, the purpose of this study is to examine whether and how EMA, the important environmental-related accounting and control factor in which

M. Aman, L. Lucianetti, *Corporate Environmental Performance and Environmental Management Accounting Systems*, SIDREA Series in Accounting and Business Administration, https://doi.org/10.1007/978-3-031-84947-3_1

organizations widely have sought its support, mediates and/or moderates the relationship between environmental governance and environmental performance.

The increasing global focus on environmental practices and the growing attention of stakeholders to environmental issues are leading companies to become more aware of the benefits of implementing environmental governance measures and mechanisms (Michelon et al., 2015).[1] This is supported by international organizations like the World Economic Forum (WEF), which has suggested that considering ecological factors at the board level is a key indicator of a firm's commitment to addressing sustainability issues and reflective of their environmental performance (WEF, 2019). As a result, companies are implementing various environmental governance mechanisms to oversee climate change issues as a strategic means for the board to meet stakeholders' expectations and monitor environmental performance (Rodrigue et al., 2013).

One consequence of this trend is the need to expand accounting practices to effectively measure environmental performance and evaluate the organization's related practices and behaviors (Qian et al., 2018). Currently, many firms are using EMA as a tool to track and improve environmental performance. This includes identifying possibilities for reducing carbon emissions and potential cost savings (Asiri et al., 2020).

EMA is broadly defined as a technique to promote and use financial and non-financial information to support decision-makers in achieving the firm objectives while paving the way for sustainable business in the form of green or environmentally friendly activities (Bartolomeo et al., 2000). Typically, EMA involves the identification, collection, analysis, reporting, and use of physical data regarding the utilization, flow, and outcome of environmental aspects (such as energy, water, and materials, relevant waste) as well as monetary aspects (including costs, revenues, and savings associated with the environment) for decision-making purposes (Burritt et al., 2002).

The use of EMA systems may provide visibility into operational activities that are often overlooked in traditional accounting, which primarily focuses on profitability and ignores environmental aspects (Qian et al., 2018). While the implementation of such practices and measures is likely to impact environmental performance, previous studies have not reached a consensus on the relationship between environmental governance and EMA. Additionally, they have not expanded their analysis to include corporate environmental performance (Ghosh & Wolf, 2021; Gunarathne et al., 2021; Qian et al., 2018). This issue requires further exploration to determine whether EMA affects the governance-performance relationship and to what extent. Therefore, we are conducting an empirical analysis to examine the mediating and moderating effect of EMA on the relationship between environmental governance and corporate environmental performance in Italian firms. This presents an excellent opportunity to contribute new insights to mainstream corporate environmental

[1] Environmental governance can be defined as a "set of regulatory processes, mechanisms, and organizations through which policy actors influence environmental actions and outcomes" (Fisher et al., 2021).

literature. Our analysis is informed by theoretical insights from the firm's natural resource-based view (NRBV) and stakeholder theories.

The ways in which organizations can turn their environmental resources into better performance are not very clear (Gunarathne et al., 2021). Since environmental governance mechanisms work together to influence management decisions, it is important to understand how they collectively impact environmental performance. It is possible that companies could improve their managerial monitoring by using strong and adaptable governance mechanisms to bring in diverse viewpoints, ideas, perspectives, and abilities during the decision-making process, leading to better performance (Albitar et al., 2023). Therefore, the adoption of EMA can impact the relationship between environmental governance and environmental performance (Gerged et al., 2024; Latan et al., 2018; Lisi, 2015).

The study examines the impact of EMA on corporate environmental performance. In today's competitive business environment, companies have been utilizing environmental-related accounting and effective control systems and strategies to improve their environmental performance (Burritt et al., 2019). Gunarathne and Lee (2021) also suggest that implementing the EMA system can be a critical component in achieving a sustainable environmental strategy model and environmental performance improvement by timely reporting on each phase of the product and its environmental impact. However, despite the growing interest in corporate environmental management strategies and supporting accounting systems, there is currently a lack of empirical evidence on whether the implementation of these systems, such as EMA, can improve corporate environmental performance (Gunarathne et al., 2021; Latan et al., 2018). Consequently, there are still persistent gaps in the literature, including the role of the firm's internal management systems, like EMA, in improving environmental performance.

The study focuses on samples from FTSE firms listed on the Italian Stock Exchange. These firms are considered to be leading organizations in disclosing their sustainable development goals and practices (SDGs) within their organizational mission. They are likely to dedicate significant time and resources to reporting their social and environmental performance data (Veltri & Ferraro, 2018). The environmental data are drawn from the Thomson Reuters Refinitiv Eikon database. Financial and control data are extracted from the Aida Database developed by Bureau van Dijk. After the data collection, we conducted several empirical analyses, and we reported the main results together with a set of performed robustness checks to ensure the soundness of our statistical outcomes.

This study makes several contributions to the scientific community. Firstly, it adds to the emerging research on the connection between environmental governance and environmental performance (Bui et al., 2020; Moussa et al., 2021), environmental governance and EMA (Rodrigue et al., 2013; Shen & Chen, 2021), and EMA and environmental performance (Asiaei et al., 2021; Chaudhry & Amir, 2020; Latan et al., 2018) by examining the role of EMA in the relationship between environmental governance and environmental performance. More specifically, we empirically examine how EMA can mediate and moderate the relationship between corporate environmental performance and environmental governance mechanisms, such as sustainability assurance, sustainability committee, emission mitigation target horizon, and global reporting initiative (GRI) guidelines. This research aims to fill a gap in existing environmental studies by empirically investigating EMA's mediating and moderating effect on environmental governance and environmental performance. Additionally, our study introduces findings from the Italian context, as Italy's economy is one of the largest in the Eurozone. This area of inquiry has previously produced inconsistent results.

Therefore, this study is an attempt to bridge the existing gap in the literature. The research study is going to address the following questions.

1. What are the impacts of environmental governance on environmental performance?
2. What are the influences of EMA on environmental performances?
3. What is the mediating impact of EMA on the relationship between environmental governance and environmental performances?
4. What is the moderating impact of EMA on the relationship between environmental governance and environmental performances?

The book consists of five chapters that include an introduction and outline the main conclusions. The work can be divided into two main parts. The first part highlights the literature review of the considered topics. The first part consists of three chapters and is organized as follows: After the introduction, in Chap. 2, we outline the conceptualization and evolution of corporate environmental performance. In the next sections, we explore the environmental performance measurements and capture the impact on the disclosure practices in the literature. Moreover, we emphasize the purpose and implication of environmental performance measurement systems. In the last section of the chapter, we highlight the overlaps between environmental accounting and corporate accountability. Chapter 3 describes the concept of environmental management accounting, outlining the evolution of EMA, the main tools, and the consequences of adoption.

The second part of the study concerns the empirical studies of integrating environmental governance mechanisms and corporate environmental performance into environmental management accounting systems. This part is organized as follows: In Chap. 4, we develop the theoretical framework and hypotheses development in the first section of the chapter. The research method employed in the study is demonstrated in the following section. In addition, we analyzed and discussed the empirical results. The final remarks are presented in Chap. 5, including managerial implications, suggested directions for future research, and study limitations.

Chapter 2
Corporate Environmental Performance and Environmental Disclosure

This chapter describes corporate environmental performance and the frameworks for its disclosure. The chapter begins in Sect. 2.1, where corporate environmental performance is defined and conceptualized, establishing a foundation for understanding its role within organizations. Section 2.2 presents an overview of corporate environmental performance as a multidimensional construct, highlighting the various facets through which it can be assessed and analyzed. Section 2.3 shows the role of environmental management control systems in facilitating the transparent disclosure of corporate environmental information, emphasizing their importance for organizational accountability. Subsections within this section further explore specific mechanisms: Sect. 2.3.1 addresses the purpose and implications of environmental performance measurement systems, while Sect. 2.3.2 discusses the role of environmental accounting in enhancing corporate accountability.

2.1 Conceptualization and Definition of Corporate Environmental Performance

Like most other phenomena in organizational research, corporate environmental performance cannot be observed directly and, therefore, has to be viewed as a construct (Trumpp et al., 2015). Accordingly, the construct is thus connected to observable reality through indicators or measures, which refer to a concept's visible manifestations or aspects. A frequently used approach for comprehending a construct is to examine how the construct has been addressed in the literature (Combs et al., 2005). In this respect, Gilley et al. (2000) stated that "Without a common definition and measure of environmental performance, our understanding of its antecedents and consequences will be hindered." Despite the emerging research stream concerned with the significance of corporate performance measurement in the

M. Aman, L. Lucianetti, *Corporate Environmental Performance and Environmental Management Accounting Systems*, SIDREA Series in Accounting and Business Administration, https://doi.org/10.1007/978-3-031-84947-3_2

environmental context, the definition of environmental performance is not seen as an easy task (Ilinitch et al., 1998). This is primarily because the vast majority of studies do not offer a unified and widely accepted definition of corporate environmental performance; aspects of operationalization and scope are still lacking (Asiaei et al., 2023; Trumpp et al., 2015). In an attempt to provide a comprehensive conceptualization of corporate environmental performance and to solve the dilemma of how exactly to measure environmental performance, the dedicated literature provides a number of definitions of environmental performance from diverse perspectives and contexts. For instance, some studies provide definitions from a narrow perspective, such as emissions and water pollution (Mungai et al., 2020). Others advocate a broader perspective, such as Judge and Douglas (1998), who illustrate environmental performance as "a firm's effectiveness in meeting and exceeding society's expectations with respect to concerns for the natural environment."

Other studies refer to the definition introduced by environmental organizations such as the International Organization for Standardization (ISO) 14031, which describes environmental performance as "the measurable results related to the management of environmental aspects" (ISO, 2013). According to Trumpp et al. (2015), this definition is considered comprehensive, succinct, and widely accepted as it encompasses the essential aspects of the environmental effects of management activities as well as those activities themselves. In comparison to academic viewpoints and ISO 14031, the authors distinguish between two pillars of environmental performance: environmental operational performance and environmental management performance. The former is mostly quantitative, covering inputs and outputs, regulatory compliance, and other environmental information related to product and service performance. The latter focuses on qualitative aspects such as policy, objectives, processes, organizational structure, and monitoring.

Although the concept meaning under the ISO definition is considered broad and concise, it is obscured by the term "environmental aspects" with no clear conceptual boundaries. Dragomir (2018) conceptualizes environmental performance with respect to its impacts, not general aspects. The impacts are to be measurable, managed, and reduced negative impacts of operational activities on the environment. Then, the author defined corporate environmental performance as a measure of environmental impacts, resource consumption, other related expenditures, and the efforts to minimize such impacts. The definition includes the key environmental measurement dimensions that assess the operational effects of a program and other metrics used by organizations to evaluate performance efficiency. Operational impact encompasses performance related to inputs (e.g., water, materials, and energy), outputs (e.g., solid waste, effluents, and carbon emissions), and other relevant environmental-related information. The definition specifically addresses the dimensions of inputs, outputs, environmental compliance, and other economic-related information. From this perspective, the measurement, prevention, and reduction of impacts are integrated within a comprehensive management system that involves both corporate insiders and external stakeholders. Therefore, corporate environmental performance is not only contingent upon compliance with existing requirements but also on proactive community activities and continual engagement with stakeholders.

2.2 Corporate Environmental Performance: A Multidimensional Construct

When we attempt to measure a multidimensional construct, we face several dilemmas (Dragomir, 2018).

A multidimensional construct refers to a theoretical concept comprising several interconnected dimensions that can be conceptually represented under a meaningful overall abstraction (Law et al., 1998). When dealing with multidimensional constructs, it is essential to specify the various dimensions that make up the entire construct. As discussed earlier, Trumpp et al. (2015) conducted a review linking the ISO 14001 framework and academic perspectives on the main dimensions of corporate environmental performance. They identified two primary dimensions: environmental management performance (EMP) and environmental operational performance (EOP), where EMP is qualitative and EOP is mostly qualitative. The EMP dimension pertains to the strategic aspect of environmental performance, emphasizing management principles and practices concerning the natural environment. On the other hand, the EOP dimension pertains to the operational level of environmental performance, specifically centering on the measurable outcomes (i.e., environmental aspects) resulting from a firm's environmental management practices. These dimensions are interconnected since EOP reflects the measurable results stemming from the EMP dimensions initiatives in managing the natural environment.

EMP includes sub-dimensions such as environmental policy, objectives, processes, organizational structure and governance, and monitoring. On the other hand, EOP includes environmental results, inputs, outputs, regulatory compliance, and environmental performance of products and services (eco-balance analysis). Apart from EMP and EOP, other dimensions like customer satisfaction, stakeholder relations, financial issues, and outcomes (financial, non-financial) could be assigned to neither firm management activities nor environmental outputs, which are encompassed under the term "environmental condition" by ISO 14001.

However, Dragomir introduced a more integrative classification (2018) based on functional aspects of corporate environmental performance. The proposed approach, derived from Porter's value chain model (Porter, 2001), focuses on the main corporate functions, not just the physical nature of environmental impacts. It identifies and addresses environmental impacts at every stage of the business process, allowing for greater relevance to management decisions and environmental transparency for stakeholders. The classification differs from the Global Reporting Initiative's (GRI) separation, which categorizes environmental impacts into materials, energy, water, etc. It includes main economic function dimensions like recycling and clean-up programs, incidents, biodiversity impact, costs and investments in technology and payrolls associated with reduction effect, fines, penalties, and compensation. In addition, other aspects of corporate activities may also include environmental components that are secondary to their primary economic role, such as products, transportation, employee training, and supplier selection. These dimensions can be aligned with the social dimensions of the GRI Standards, which mainly address aspects like workplace health and safety, education, and local community impacts. Furthermore, assessing corporate environmental performance involves evaluating the implementation of the environmental management system, the degree of environmental compliance, the environmental governance system, and the quality of corporate environmental disclosures.

2.3 The Role of Environmental Management Control Systems to Disclose Corporate Environmental Information

2.3.1 Purpose and Implications of Environmental Performance Measurement Systems

Contemporary organizations are increasingly agreeing on the importance of strong environmental control systems. These systems help compare outcomes against predetermined objectives and improve the use of environmentally friendly resources to create more value efficiently (Ding et al., 2022). Adopting such practices and tools can help companies understand the environmental impact of their actions and communicate their sustainable value to stakeholders, thus enhancing the organization's long-term success (Qian et al., 2018). In this context, Environmental Performance Measurement Systems (referred to as EPMS) have attracted significant interest as tools for integrating environmental concerns into business processes (Dragomir, 2018; Lisi, 2015; Pham et al., 2020).

As a specialized application of performance measurement systems (PMS), EPMS is a central aspect of environmental management control systems (Henri & Journeault, 2010). They primarily provide pertinent information to facilitate effective decision-making and pave the way for achieving environmental goals through performance evaluation and recognition (Pham et al., 2020). By aligning managerial processes with organizational objectives and core value drivers, EPMS can enable organizations to translate their environmental resources and capabilities into superior performance (Lisi, 2015). The incorporation of sustainability into organizational control systems, including PMS, has been suggested to yield positive organizational outcomes (Lisi, 2015).

Before exploring the purpose and implications of EPMS, it is essential to define EPMS. The definitions of the broader terminology for "performance measurement systems" have been addressed in management accounting literature. PMS can be defined as "the set of metrics used to quantify both the efficiency and effectiveness of actions" (Neely et al., 1995). Carlsson-Wall et al. (2016) define PMS as a "set of performance measures that are jointly considered when making sense of the performance of an organization." These definitions remain a broad topic and have failed to identify the environmental aspects. The existing literature has acknowledged EPMS from various angles and perspectives. For instance, EPMs can be defined regarding their features as a system that promotes the utilization of analytical instruments that supply critical information about the environmental effect of an organization's operating processes (Journeault et al., 2016). ISO 14031 provides environmental performance evaluation guidelines that allow firms to measure, evaluate, and communicate their environmental performance using key performance indicators (KPIs) and to identify areas for development. It can be defined as a "process to facilitate management decisions regarding an organization's environmental performance by selecting indicators, collecting and analyzing data, assessing information against environmental performance criteria, reporting and communicating this to senior management and periodically reviewing and improving this process" (ISO, 2013). In addition, EPMS can be defined in respect of their impacts. For instance, Dragomir (2018) defined EPMS as an integrated management approach measuring the environmental impacts, resource consumption, and other related expenditures, as well as the efforts toward ensuring the reduction of such impacts. This process necessitates technology skills, stringent compliance, staff training, supply chain management, and stakeholder relations.

EPMS can also be defined with respect to their roles within the organization as "the extent to which managers use Environmental Performance Measures (EPM) or a variety of different purposes pertaining to both the 'decision-making' and decision-control ('decision-influencing') roles of management accounting information" (Lisi, 2015). Based on this definition, EPMS supports decision-makers in translating a broad set of environmental information and objectives into performance (Chen et al., 2023). Similarly, Perego and Hartmann (2009) conclude that EPMs are metrics and results that supply measurable information on environmental impact, governance, stakeholder communication, and organizational systems through specific expressions that illustrate the interaction between the management and the environment. A consensus is that the literature lacks a common definition, as EPM systems are analyzed from different perspectives. To circumvent this constraint and streamline our assessment, we take the approach proposed by Franco-Santos et al. (2012) in respect of emphasizing its essential and sufficient requirements. Therefore, we contend that EPMS is employed when economic, environmental, and social impacts are measured and managed to fulfill relevant strategic objectives.

The purposes behind firms engaging in performance measurement are extensively studied in the broader literature on performance assessments. This literature outlines a diverse array of objectives, including tracking progress, comprehending and appraising performance, identifying challenges and bottlenecks, finding out the root causes of problems and opportunities for change, defining new objectives and targets, validating priorities, charting future courses of action, aiding operational staff, and providing performance reports (Franco-Santos et al., 2012; Neely et al., 1995). When the scope of performance measurement extends to encompass environmental performance, numerous similar objectives emerge.

EPMS constitute essential components within environmental management control systems and represent a specific utilization of performance measurement systems (Henri & Journeault, 2010). These systems primarily supply decision-making with information and expedite the accomplishment of environmental objectives through performance evaluation and incentivization (Lisi, 2015; Perego & Hartmann, 2009). EPMS play a crucial role in assisting organizations in translating their environmental capabilities into heightened performance, given their potential to enhance the alignment between managerial processes and organizational objectives as well as underlying value drivers (Perego & Hartmann, 2009; Pham et al., 2020). Firms would achieve the long-term economic and environmental benefits that can result from employing environmental management accounting (EMA) in a general sense, with particular emphasis on EPMS. Such systems are designed and implemented to stimulate environmental performance by promoting resource efficiency, pollution prevention, stakeholder management, regulatory compliance, cost savings, and eco-innovation (Henri & Journeault, 2010; Lisi, 2015).

The academic literature shows that there is a significant link between elements of management accounting systems, particularly EPMS, and environmental performance. If EPMS is used for decision-making, it helps to integrate environmental issues into everyday business activities, reduce uncertainties, and improve environmental performance by addressing critical environmental concerns. Additionally, using EPMS for control purposes, such as performance evaluation and incentives, can promote alignment with environmental objectives among employees and the company. This encourages behavior that is in line with environmental goals, ultimately leading to improved environmental performance. Using EPMS for performance evaluation and incentives reinforces the importance of balancing both environmental and financial considerations. In summary, academic literature highlights the various benefits of performance measurement in businesses, especially when it comes to environmental performance. EPMS supports decision-making, aligns goals among employees, and balances environmental and financial considerations, all of which contribute to improved corporate environmental performance (Lisi, 2015).

2.3.2 Environmental Accounting and Corporate Accountability

Environmental performance measures (EPM) share several roles with traditional management accounting (Qian et al., 2018). These roles include setting objectives, providing information to decision-makers, reporting, and monitoring compliance (Gunarathne & Lee, 2015). EMA and control systems are expected to provide a competitive advantage, which motivates managers to invest in these systems to measure their costs, benefits, and operational outcomes. Even though the various uses of EPMs within EMA have received less attention, EPMs are still a crucial part of EMA, specifically in the context of PMs (Henri & Journeault, 2010; Lisi, 2015).

EMA and EPMs play an important role in providing information for decision-makers and supporting environmental objectives through performance evaluation and reward (Lisi, 2015; Perego & Hartmann, 2009). Therefore, EPMs are considered a subset of EMA that quantifies an organization's environmental performance in terms of efficiency and effectiveness (Dragomir, 2018). For instance, some aspects of using one of EMA's important tools, such as the sustainability balanced scorecard, can be notable in some organizations that integrate environmental consideration with the implemented performance measurement systems.

Various environmental measurement classifications have been proposed to track how firms' environmental efforts and performance change over time. One of the main challenges is to develop a classification of EPMs that effectively captures the corporate focus on sustainability. The aim is to improve understanding of these complex systems. The balanced scorecard (BSC), a strategic management tool, has been used for environmental management implementation (Hristov et al., 2021). The BSC offers a cohesive framework that can be tailored to different types of organizations and their missions (Cooper et al., 2017). Chalmeta and Palomero (2011) suggest that integrating BSC and environmental dimensions can be achieved by designing a set of measures based on cause-and-effect relationships. This allows the organizational strategy to be translated into operational actions. EPMs can consist of both financial and non-financial measures that provide key information on the interaction between the business and the environment (Henri & Journeault, 2010).

In a study by Maas et al. (2016), it was noted that the integration of financial and non-financial information for internal performance management and management control has evolved and is captured in concepts like the sustainability balanced scorecard (SBSC). The SBSC assists in aligning sustainability components with the performance measurement system (PMS) by providing performance metrics, facilitating value creation, and improving corporate performance. The BSC, as proposed by Figge et al. (2002), provides a systematic approach to linking sustainability management to corporate strategy. Developing an SBSC ensures the integration of environmental, social, and economic performance. According to the requirements, the process can be broken down into three steps: first, identifying strategic business objectives; second, recognizing environmental and social aspects; and finally, determining the link between the strategy and environmental and social aspects.

The EMA primarily focuses on the environmental issues arising from operational activities. The SBSC serves as a link between performance management systems (PMS) that rely on key performance indicators (KPIs) and sustainability factors. Its goal is to add value and enhance organizational performance (Hubbard, 2009). As the primary tool of EMA, the SBSC meets the strategic needs of organizations for sustainable development by providing management with information on all dimensions of sustainability. It achieves this by integrating financial data and considering non-monetary environmental and social aspects (Figge et al., 2002).

Previous research has explored EPMs and their implications for sustainable performance management. Based on existing literature, we can categorize the consequences of EPMs according to their composition and specific purposes. EPMs are comprised of financial and non-financial performance measures that are aligned with strategic environmental objectives, and they also emphasize cause-and-effect relationships between environmental measures and performance measures (PMs). According to Günther and Kaulich (2005), EPMs involve recording and evaluating a company's environmental outcomes. Thus, the primary goal of EPMs is to integrate environmental concerns into regulations and procedures, leading to improved environmental performance.

Additionally, EPMs facilitate decision-making by establishing cause-and-effect relationships among environmental processes, initiatives, and goals. This strategic coherence and environmental alignment allow firms to embed sustainable development into their corporate models and decision-making processes early in the performance management system (PMS) cycle (Dutta et al., 2013). Consequently, EMA is a valuable tool for managers, enabling cost reduction, operational efficiency, and product improvement. Ultimately, the purpose of EPMs is to provide decision-makers with information that addresses their concerns and evaluates the performance of environmental management processes in achieving organizational objectives (Table 2.1).

Research on environmental accounting and EPMS is still being developed. Previous studies did not clearly distinguish between the two concepts (Ferreira et al., 2010; Mokhtar et al., 2016; Perego & Hartmann, 2009). This becomes more challenging as the field is constantly changing, and scholars and organizations are trying to define and understand how integration could be modeled and executed efficiently (Dragomir, 2018; Morioka & Carvalho, 2016; Qian et al., 2018). Even though there are various theories and empirical research, best practices are still being debated.

This research focuses on the relationship between corporate environmental performance, disclosure, governance, and EMA practices. It is important to give an overview of the environmental management and accounting literature to outline the concepts and assumptions that form the theoretical framework. The next chapter will discuss EMA practices as part of an environmental management control system to maintain or improve CEP and disclosure. It will be organized into four sections.

Table 2.1 Classification of the EPM inspired by the work of Franco-Santos et al. (2012)

	EPM A	EPM B	EPM C
Composition	• Financial performance measures and non-financial performance measures linked to the strategic environmental goals,	• Financial performance measures and non-financial performance measures linked to the strategic environmental goals. • Finding cause-and-effect alignment between the environmental performance measures.	• Financial performance measures and non-financial performance measures linked to the strategic environmental goals.
Specific purpose	• Provide support for decision-making. • Represent and evaluate the corresponding environmental impacts of corporate decisions and performance.	• Provide support for decision-making. • Represent and evaluate the corresponding environmental impacts of corporate decisions and performance.	• Provide support for decision-making. • Represent and evaluate the corresponding environmental impacts of corporate decisions and performance in relation to the incentive system.

Section one will define the EMA concept and explain what is usually referred to by the term 'environmental management accounting.' Sections two and three will discuss the literature on EMA frameworks as the next step in the evolution of management accounting practices to manage environmental matters. Section four will highlight the principles of EMA and discuss the EMA tools and their application to various aspects of organizational environmental management. Finally, section five will discuss the literature on the consequences of EMA implementation and the links between EMA and performance, providing insights into the potential role of environmental governance in the environmental management arena.

Chapter 3
Environmental Management Accounting Practices

This chapter focuses on EMA practices, a critical area within corporate sustainability efforts and essential to creating a situation in which the organization handles various environmental problems proactively. Critical undertakings such as environmental preservation and environmentally aware actions should be an integral part of the overall corporate strategy. Section 3.1 starts by defining the concept of EMA, as well as setting the basis for understanding its scope and objectives within organizational contexts. Section 3.2 shows the evolution of EMA practices, examining how these approaches have developed over time to meet shifting regulatory, societal, and corporate demands. Section 3.3 presents a structured decision framework for EMA, offering guidance on how organizations can integrate environmental considerations into their decision-making regarding financial, non-financial, and operational activities. Section 3.4 details the tools of EMA that organizations can use to understand environmental management and incorporation in business activities. Finally, Sect. 3.5 unveils the impact of EMA implementation and its tools on environmental management, addressing how these practices influence corporate transparency and accountability and what should be understood when implementing the tools to manage any company's environmental and accounting activities.

3.1 Defining the Concept of Environmental Management Accounting

In the literature, several terms are used to describe similar concepts. For example, "eco-control" is defined as the integration of a firm's financial and accounting procedures (financial control), the establishment and implementation of performance standards, the evaluation of current performance, and the formulation of strategic plans for long-term business growth (strategic control) with an environmental

M. Aman, L. Lucianetti, *Corporate Environmental Performance and Environmental Management Accounting Systems*, SIDREA Series in Accounting and Business Administration, https://doi.org/10.1007/978-3-031-84947-3_3

management system (Henri & Journeault, 2010). "Environmental management control system" (EMCS) is defined as "A set of formal procedures used by managers to maintain or change patterns of organizational activities, particularly regarding environmental aspects" (Pondeville et al., 2013). "Environmental performance measurement system" refers to the use of EPM by managers in the decision-making process and decision-making control roles related to management accounting information (Lisi, 2015). Finally, environmentally friendly practices are also known as EMA (Gunarathne & Lee, 2015).

EMA is a broad term; many scholars have given a diversity of definitions and different perspectives. For example, some consider it as a technique to promote and use financial and non-financial information to support decision-makers in achieving the firm's environmental or economic objectives (Burritt et al., 2019). However, the United Nations Division of Sustainable Development (UNDSD) defines EMA as a comprehensive approach that demonstrates the hidden costs of identifying, collecting, evaluating, analyzing, and then reporting physical information, environmental costs, and other monetary information for the interested parties (UNDSD, 2001). On the other hand, the International Federation of Accountants (IFAC) defines EMA as the management of monetary EMA information (economic) and—physical EMA information (environmental) to gauge performance through developing and implementing the appropriate system, which encompasses accounting and environmental practice (IFAC, 2005).

The widely accepted definition for EMA is a technique to promote and use financial and non-financial information to support decision-makers in achieving the firm objectives while paving the way for sustainable business in the form of green or environmentally friendly activities (Bartolomeo et al., 2000). In this regard, the EMA application process entails specific procedures and drivers at which the organization responds to its external environment efficiently and expeditiously (Latan et al., 2018). In a more specific sense, EMA plays a vital role in achieving environmental goals and understanding their commitments by minimizing firms' operational activities that negatively impact the environment (Burritt et al., 2019). In addition, as a key dimension of sustainability accounting, EMA is an important tool in informing the organization about the practices with respect to the environment and the financial aspects that aim to minimize costs and reduce energy consumption and waste. In this regard, EMA is helpful for the management in measuring, monitoring, and disseminating firms' environmental performance and sustainable development (Qian et al., 2018). The more advanced the use of EMA, the better the decision quality and effective organizational control will be, and the more intensified impact on corporate environmental performance (Chaudhry & Amir, 2020).

In summary, it is worth noting that there is no universally accepted definition and terminology despite a widespread understanding of EMA over the past decade (IFAC, 2005). Furthermore, research on EMA is still developing (Mokhtar et al., 2016).

EMA is broadly defined as a technique to promote and use financial and non-financial information to support decision-makers in achieving the firm's objectives while paving the way for sustainable business in the form of green or environmentally friendly activities (Bartolomeo et al., 2000). Typically, EMA involves the identification, collection, analysis, reporting, and use of physical data regarding the utilization, flow, and outcome of environmental aspects (such as energy, water, and materials, relevant waste) as well as monetary aspects (including costs, revenues, and savings associated with the environment) for decision-making purposes (Burritt et al., 2002). The latter definition of EMA and the following applications of EMA tools emphasize two key aspects of EMA information: (1) Initially, EMA systems provide data concerning diverse 'environmental aspects,' including energy, water, materials, carbon, waste, and biodiversity. (2) Subsequently, the data provided by EMA is applied across diverse 'organizational decision-making' contexts, i.e., for different purposes and objectives.

Nonetheless, there is a lack of unified consensus and confusion to differentiate between EMA, environmental management system (EMS), and environmental management control system (EMCS), even among some scholars who have published in the field (Asiaei et al., 2021). The term environmental management accounting and the comprehensive definition provided by Burritt et al. (2002) are considered for the study.

3.2 The Evolutions of Environmental Management Accounting Practice

The concept of EMA emerged as a response to the need for sustainable development (Bartolomeo et al., 2000). In the early 1990s, the Environmental Protection Agency (EPA) in the United States promoted the adoption of EMA practices, leading to its widespread use by organizations worldwide to address environmental concerns (EPA, 1995). In 2005, the International Federation of Accountants (IFAC) published guidelines for EMA research and implementation, providing a key resource for EMA-related research and implications (Ferreira et al., 2010). EMA is primarily used to help businesses manage natural resources, energy, and waste, as well as to identify costs associated with environmental impact (Johnstone, 2020). Its primary goal is to guide organizations towards eco-efficiency and sustainable development.

EMA is increasingly being recognized as a crucial tool for organizations to achieve success by integrating environmental considerations into their business operations. In today's business world, success is not only measured by profit but also by how well an organization acknowledges and supports the fundamental elements of societal progress (Lisi, 2015). Environmental preservation has become a pivotal determinant of an organization's success (Wang et al., 2018). As a result, many businesses have adopted practices aimed at reducing environmental pollution and promoting cleaner production processes to enhance corporate social responsibility. In traditional business contexts, there is a reciprocal relationship between the environment and business activities, with each exerting influence on the other. Therefore, it is essential for firms to establish robust measures and mitigation strategies to reduce their environmental footprint and address the impact on their sustained existence in society. EMA can be seen as a solution to help firms understand the impact of environmental practices on their operational dynamics. It serves as a tool for organizations to gain insights into their environmental performance, including metrics such as energy consumption, water utilization, and physical space usage (Sands & Lee, 2015).

As stated by Sharma and Vredenburg (1998), EMA enhances organizational performance by improving operations, reputation, and competitive advantage through proactive management of environmental issues. It also provides insights into the associated costs of these environmental factors. This information is essential for organizations as it allows them to evaluate their environmental management strategies thoroughly. EMA also encourages managers to seek relevant information regarding factors affecting both the industry's financial and environmental performance while ensuring compliance with environmental regulations (Asiri et al., 2020). Furthermore, it empowers them to make well-informed decisions for enhancing and refining areas that require adjustment, thus leading to more effective integration of environmental considerations into their organizational framework.

3.3 The Development of a Comprehensive Decision Framework for Environmental Management Accounting

As discussed earlier, EMA provides both physical information and monetary insights regarding the utilization and flow of resources like energy, water, and materials, alongside financial information concerning environmental costs, revenues, and savings. This has given rise to two distinct types of EMA systems: Monetary EMA (MEMA) and physical EMA (PEMA). MEMA primarily deals with quantifying the environmental effects of corporate operations in monetary terms, whereas PEMA assesses a firm's environmental footprint using physical units. Moreover, EMA distinguishes between ad hoc and routine information, focusing on past, present, and future timeframes and considering both short-term and long-term perspectives.

Building on these dimensions of EMA information, Schaltegger et al. (1996) proposed the earlier framework for EMA, then Burritt et al. (2002) developed an integrative framework for EMA and possible tools that can be used. The nature of administrative decision-making varies between short-term operational decisions and long-term investment decisions. It involves fiscal and physical measures such as material flow accounting, environmental cost accounting, budgeting, eco-investment accounting, and performance measurements. Managers need four types of information to make decisions—fiscal or physical, future-oriented or past-oriented, short or long-term, and constant or ad-hoc. By using these elements, managers can evaluate investment projects and plan finances effectively (Tsui, 2014). Furthermore, a comprehensive framework for EMA includes fiscal elements like environmental cost accounting, fiscal assessment of environmental project investments, costing, returns, and savings (life cycle costing), and environmental budgeting and planning. Physical elements include material flow cost accounting, physical assessment of environmental project investments (life cycle assessment), physical environmental budgeting and planning, and environmental performance measurements and indicators, such as EPI scorecards and incentive systems (Burritt et al., 2002).

To recapitulate, EMA constitutes a subset of environmental management accounting primarily concerned with the costs associated with environmental issues, particularly material wastage (Burritt et al., 2019). EMA endeavors to enhance organizational performance in both environmental and financial dimensions (Johnstone, 2020). This tool provides indispensable information that facilitates decision-making concerning matters intersecting environmental management and financial planning in organizations (Gunarathne & Lee, 2015). Thus, it empowers organizations to act proactively in environmental affairs.

EMA frameworks encompass two critical dimensions: financial operations and the physical environment (Burritt et al., 2002). Concerning the physical environment, EMA influences various aspects of organizational operations, including waste management, recycling, and environmental conservation techniques like energy and water consumption (Johnstone, 2020). In terms of financial aspects, the EMA framework impacts organizational financial management by examining various environmental-related costs, such as the expenses associated with cost-saving strategies for environmental operations. The EMA framework offers a wide range of management and cost-related information. In terms of management information, EMA helps managers plan and estimate costs related to various environmental activities of the organization (Burritt et al., 2019). It also tracks how the organization uses environmental resources like water and electricity and the associated costs (Latan et al., 2018). EMA functions as a tool for organizations to integrate environmental considerations into their management framework. Cost control strategies include identifying prevention costs, appraisal costs, and internal and external costs related to the organization's environmental issues.

3.4 Categories and Tools in Environmental Management Accounting

Environmental EMA encompasses diverse tools that organizations can employ to comprehend and incorporate environmental considerations into their business activities. The significance and impact of these tools vary, contingent upon the specific context within which an organization operates. These tools exhibit variations in scope and functionality and thus yield differing outcomes regarding the organization's environmental management efforts. The repertoire of EMA tools encompasses environmental assessment tools, ecological cost control models, eco-control models, environmental reporting tools, environmental appraisal tools, and environmental auditing tools (Qian et al., 2018). A pivotal challenge for organizations lies in comprehending these tools, their roles, and their repercussions as they endeavor to implement EMA in their operations (Gunarathne et al., 2023). A thorough understanding of these main EMA tools empowers organizations to determine the optimal approach for EMA implementation and the most effective strategies to employ. All of these strategies are geared towards ensuring that these tools are utilized to the fullest extent for the enhancement of environmental operations and integration into the organizational strategy.

The tools used in EMA play a crucial role in evaluating the environmental impact of industries, which directly affects organizations. For example, environmental assessment tools provide insight into important environmental issues that need to be addressed for improved environmental operations (Burritt et al., 2019). Eco-control tools help organizations understand the financial impact of environmental issues and guide effective cost management while maintaining top-notch operations (Henri & Journeault, 2010). Environmental auditing tools can be used to examine an organization's financial records related to environmental management, allowing them to assess the costs and benefits of environmental management. Additionally, environmental quality control and appraisal tools help organizations understand the benefits of their environmental activities and identify the necessary environmental adjustments for improved operations (Christ & Burritt, 2013). Understanding these tools can greatly assist organizations in successfully implementing EMA.

Despite the imperative need to comprehend and integrate EMA tools, limited research focuses on these tools. Existing literature primarily revolves around EMA's significance as a response to environmental pressures exerted by legal authorities and external stakeholders. Additionally, the literature emphasizes the importance of EMA as a tool for environmental management and explores strategies for its effective implementation. However, there is a conspicuous knowledge gap concerning the consequences of the main EMA tools (Gerged et al., 2024). Successfully adopting EMA mandates that organizations comprehend the changes required and the implications of their decisions when incorporating various EMA tools into their strategies (Christ & Burritt, 2013). Therefore, understanding the consequences of embracing eco-control, environmental auditing, environmental appraisal, assessment, and cost control is pivotal for devising more effective implementation strategies.

EMA encompasses diverse tools aimed at assisting managers in acquiring pertinent information to inform various aspects of the industry's financial and environmental performance. These tools exhibit variations in their applicability depending on the organization's context but share common objectives when applied in different organizational settings. An example of such a tool is the environmental assessment tool, employed to evaluate the costs associated with environmental approaches and the organization's performance in various environmental facets. Another critical EMA tool is eco-control, which is instrumental for organizations (Henri & Journeault, 2010). It enables the measurement, control, and accounting of environmental performance. Through this tool, organizations can manage consumption costs and expenditures associated with environmental activities.

Environmental auditing is another pivotal EMA tool essential for analyzing the extent of costs incurred by organizations. It also aids in identifying discrepancies related to environmental expenditures (Qian et al., 2018). Additionally, it proves useful in assessing income versus expenditure concerning environmental aspects within the organization (Hanif et al., 2023). Reporting and planning tools, as core EMA instruments, provide organizations with valuable information on how to manage their environment (Christ & Burritt, 2013). However, the roles of these tools have not been exhaustively discussed, necessitating an understanding of the benefits and potential adverse consequences associated with their usage (Hanif et al., 2023). Therefore, one of the aims of this research study is to unveil some of these consequences. Importantly, these consequences underpin the rationale for implementing these tools. The next section aims to elucidate both the positive and negative consequences and highlight what organizations must grasp when incorporating these tools into their environmental and accounting practices.

3.5 Consequences of Environmental Management Accounting Implementation in Environmental Management

The literature discusses several important tools for EMA. These tools include assessment tools, which help businesses determine the costs associated with different environmental activities (Christ & Burritt, 2013). Environmental accounting assessment tools focus on identifying the expenses incurred in carrying out various tasks within the organization. Another widely discussed tool is control tools (Gunarathne & Lee, 2021). Eco-control tools are used to evaluate, manage, and measure various environmental activities within the company (Gunarathne et al., 2023). They have diverse applications, including understanding consumption costs, waste management, and implementing cost reduction strategies to minimize their impact on the company's finances. Environmental auditing tools are used for accountability (Maas et al., 2016). Flow cost accounting is another essential tool for organizations, providing transparency in material costs and facilitating a better understanding of their expenses and benefits (Christ & Burritt, 2013).

Activity-based accounting is yet another tool organizations can rely on to track their diverse environmental activities and account for their use and associated costs. Environmental accounting planning tools allow organizations to strategize efficient environmental resource management, minimizing waste (Qian et al., 2018). This includes practices like reuse, recycling, and resource reduction. Reporting tools serve as a means to communicate an organization's environmental performance, highlighting areas of success and those needing improvement, such as waste or overspending in specific areas (Gunarathne et al., 2023).

These tools also signal where additional resources may be required for specific environmental needs within the organization. The environmental accounting appraisal tool is commonly used by organizations to identify potential threats and opportunities related to the environment (Qian et al., 2018). These may encompass new regulations that present either opportunities or threats to the organization. These tools help organizations identify and prepare to mitigate threats or seize opportunities (Burritt et al., 2019).

The consequences of these tools can be either positive or negative, contingent on the organization's implementation approach (Hanif et al., 2023). Success largely hinges on allocating adequate resources to ensure positive outcomes. Numerous positive consequences arise from implementing EMA tools. Firstly, organizations become proactive in addressing environmental concerns, aligning with the growing importance of environmentally sensitive practices in modern business (Hanif et al., 2023). In modern business, stakeholders look beyond mere achievements and scrutinize organizations for their efforts in creating an overall awareness of a better society. With the escalating global environmental issues, proactive environmental management is essential (Henri & Journeault, 2010). Assessment and appraisal tools enable organizations to identify environmental threats and opportunities, scanning both internal and external environments to detect environmental-related risks and act preemptively. In addition to proactivity, better cost management emerges as another positive consequence of EMA tools. These tools inform organizations about environmental and financial activities, enabling them to minimize waste and save costs (Burritt et al., 2002). Enhanced financial accountability for environmental initiatives is critical for comprehending their impact within the organization. EMA tools, such as environmental accounting auditing, facilitate the evaluation of the effects of environmental activities on the firm accounts, allowing for precise accounting that firms can account for and recommendations to mitigate negative impacts. Environmental cost accounting aids in reducing expenses, freeing up resources for other areas (Qian et al., 2018). These tools help organizations document all costs associated with environmental initiatives, including those related to water conservation and air pollution management.

A segment environmental accounting tool is a tool that an organization can use to map out all its environmental activities, assess them, and select the best that is worth their investments. The segment accounting tool consists of both assessment and appraisal accounting techniques (Qian et al., 2018). The organization can use these techniques and tools to assess the need to adopt specific environmental control or management strategies (Sands & Lee, 2015). The segment EMA tool thus has an impact on better planning for the organization. It also facilitates better and more sensitive pro-action where the organization identifies the best environmental-related activity to invest in (Wang et al., 2018). Therefore, it has a positive consequence in the organization's environmental accounting management. It reduces the level of risk involved while making investments in any environmental-related activity within the firm. Furthermore, while using EMA tools, organizations have an opportunity to inform the public about their efforts in environmental protection and accountability

(Burritt et al., 2019). Corporate Environmental Accounting, often referred to as corporate environmental reporting, compiles an organization's environmental activities, serving as a means to communicate these efforts to the public (Latan et al., 2018). This boosts the corporate image, enhancing loyalty.

Another tool is eco-balance environmental accounting, which influences the organization and is linked to environmental sustainability (Deegan, 2017). The tool's effectiveness in the organization is that it allows the organization to plan, do, check, and act (PDAC). The process of integrating environmental accounting into the organization demands that the organization has a plan to sustain the approach and its strategies (Qian et al., 2018). Therefore, eco-balance is the EMA tool's role in creating a balance between the four elements of implementing the EMA strategy. It ensures the planning process is in balance with the pilot study, which is also cohesive with both the assessment or evaluation and implementation process (Qian et al., 2018). These ensure little waste and little risk of losses when implementing EMA.

While using EMA tools, the organization also has a chance to inform the public about some of its strategies to ensure that it protects the environment and remains accountable for operating in a safe society (Burritt et al., 2019). The EMA tool, which is critical for such a role, is Corporate Environmental Accounting. Corporate Environmental Accounting is sometimes called corporate environmental reporting. Its role is to compile all the environmental activities that the organization takes (Latan et al., 2018). The report is meant to inform the public about the organization's environmental movements. It also informs the public about the organization's role in ensuring better environmental management (Wang et al., 2018). The consequence of these tools is to increase the corporate image of the organizations. Its role is to ensure that the organization sells its activities and image to gain loyalty.

Finally, EMA remains a prudent management tool that organizations should incorporate in their undertaking to ensure better management of environmental-related activities. EMA has different critical tools for ensuring productive management and understanding of the organization's financial and environmental performance in the industry. Through these tools, the organization gets to understand where and how to invest in its environmental-related activities. The consequences of these tools are numerous. Through their application, they underline areas to invest in and how the organization should manage its environmental-related activities. They also give the organizations a blueprint regarding environmental management.

Further, they underline threats and opportunities regarding environmental issues in the industry and recommend the best and safest approaches to overcome them. By applying the EMA tools, the organization will likely understand the cost-effect relationship and take the most suitable environmental management approach. It is, therefore, advisable for organizations to apply these tools as their consequences are positive.

Chapter 4
The Relationship Between Environmental Management Accounting, Environmental Governance, and Corporate Environmental Performance: Some Empirical Evidence from Italy

This chapter examines the interconnection of environmental management accounting, environmental governance structures, and corporate environmental performance information, with empirical evidence drawn from the Italian context. Section 4.1 introduces the theoretical framework and outlines the development of hypotheses related to the study. Section 4.1.1 explores the connection between environmental governance and environmental performance, while Sect. 4.1.2 emphasizes the impact of EMA on environmental performance. Section 4.1.3 addresses the combined effects of environmental governance and EMA on environmental performance information outcomes. Section 4.2 presents the research methodology applied in the study, beginning with Sect. 4.2.1, which places the research within the Italian context. Section 4.2.2 describes the sample and data collection procedures, followed by Sect. 4.2.3, which specifics the measurement of variables. Section 4.2.4 provides descriptive statistics, Sect. 4.2.5 includes the correlation matrix, and Sect. 4.2.6 concludes with a presentation and discussion of regression results, offering insights into the observed relationships. We provide a battery of robustness tests that are performed to ensure the reliability of our results, and overall, the tests support the robustness of our findings.

4.1 Theoretical Framework and Hypothesis Development

The association between environmental governance, environmental management accounting, and corporate environmental performance is a complex topic that a single theory cannot fully explain. To address this complexity, our study combines the firm's natural resource-based view and stakeholder theory to create a framework model. By integrating these theoretical perspectives, we can better understand the

M. Aman, L. Lucianetti, *Corporate Environmental Performance and Environmental Management Accounting Systems*, SIDREA Series in Accounting and Business Administration, https://doi.org/10.1007/978-3-031-84947-3_4

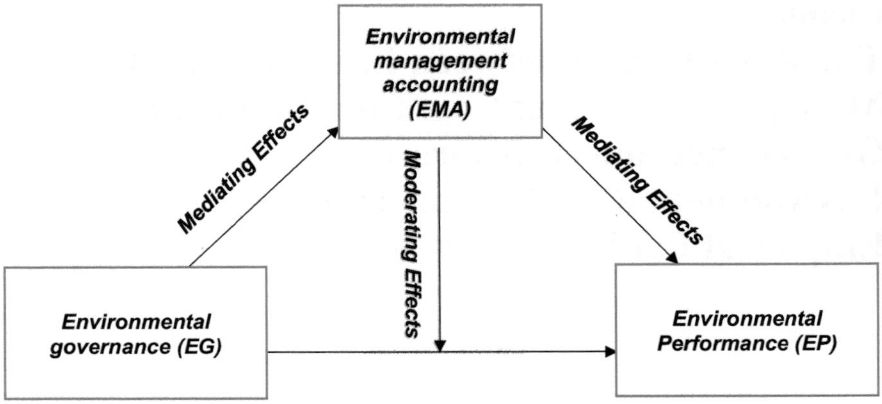

Fig. 4.1 Theoretical framework. Source: Authors' own work

role of EMA in linking environmental governance mechanisms and environmental performance, as outlined in our theoretical framework (Fig. 4.1).

The natural resource-based view (NRBV) emphasizes the importance of natural resources in a firm's overall environmental strategies, a factor that traditional theories overlook (Haque, 2017). The theory proposes that a company's strategy and competitive advantage should be based on internal capabilities that support environmentally friendly economic activities (Hart, 1995). This idea is built on the assumption that a competitive advantage can only be maintained if the ability to generate profits is supported by resources that are hard for competitors to replicate. In other words, while being environmentally conscious may strain a company's resources, continuous improvements in environmental strategy can guide businesses toward sustainable development (Brooks & Oikonomou, 2018).

Companies can promote environmental protection through three interconnected environmental strategies (Hart, 1995). First, they can focus on pollution prevention throughout the production process by responsibly managing waste. Second, they can work on reducing greenhouse gas emissions using advanced methods and technologies. Third, they can engage in sustainable practices by using fewer components to manufacture their products and decommissioning them at the end of their life cycle for recycling or reuse. Therefore, companies need to build up resources and manage their capacities with a long-term perspective rather than prioritizing only short-term profits in order to respond to the natural environment and achieve ongoing environmental performance success (Boakye et al., 2021).

As such, improving environmental performance will benefit corporate reputation, increasing the capacity to manage its resources more effectively (Latan et al., 2018). In other words, a better reputation implies that the combination of resources and competencies across all firm areas will be more profitable (Rodrigue et al., 2013). In a nutshell, NRBV claims that an organization can continue to make profits and maintain a competitive advantage in the market through efficient resource management, which also contributes to waste elimination, pollution prevention, promotion of environmentally friendly products, and continuous mitigation of mechanisms that degrade the environment (Latan et al., 2018).

In the same vein, the stakeholder theory is frequently discussed in environmental research. It is generally believed that stakeholders can impact an organization's operations by exerting pressure on them. As competition increases, having better connections with stakeholders may benefit firms (Boakye et al., 2021). Stakeholders, including regulators, clients, environmental groups, media, and shareholders, have diverse information demands. It is essential for firms to meet these demands based on the relevance of the desired data and the stakeholders involved (Asiri et al., 2020). As a result, firms face a combination of regulatory and stakeholder pressures as they become more focused on achieving overall performance in both financial and environmental aspects rather than just progressing in an organizational context (Friedman, 1984).

Research suggests that stakeholders perceive their company as having a strong commitment to environmental responsibility when management prioritizes long-term environmental goals over short-term profitability (Li et al., 2020). According to Clarkson et al. (2008), companies should take proactive measures to address environmental issues to achieve their long-term objectives. Therefore, in order to emphasize sustainable practices, companies aim to meet the needs of stakeholders by integrating social and environmental considerations into their operations. These companies should focus on managing their operations effectively to demonstrate high performance and accountability to stakeholders, taking into account the importance of different stakeholder groups in providing necessary resources (Friedman, 1984). Consequently, companies should take necessary precautions to prevent the continuation of unsustainable practices that could have a negative ecological impact (Marrucci et al., 2022).

Due to the fact that the board of directors is liable for the governance of their businesses, boards adopt environmental governance procedures to fulfill stakeholders' environmental expectations, handle environmental performance challenges, and monitor the firm's environmental performance (Rodrigue et al., 2013). Thus, strong environmental governance mechanisms effectively respond to stakeholder information needs and steward their interests, which can positively impact corporate environmental performance (Albitar et al., 2023). Similarly, NBRV implies that strong environmental governance mechanisms can increase pressure on firms to engage in environmentally responsible initiatives, ensuring that an organization's growth has a minimal environmental impact, thereby achieving a green image and competitive advantage. Based on the perspectives and theories mentioned above, it is suggested that effective governance mechanisms can increase pressure on corporations to implement better environmental policies and improve corporate environmental performance. This is essential to gain the support of influential stakeholders and subsequently improve resource management, leading to a competitive advantage. In summary, the combination of NRBV and stakeholder theory can explain how the use of proper management accounting systems, such as EMA, and environmental governance mechanisms can enhance corporate environmental performance based on a solid theoretical foundation.

4.1.1 Environmental Governance and Environmental Performance

Corporate governance has been traditionally taught as the rules and principles that prescribe the firm's relationship with its stakeholders (Velte, 2023). Corporate governance is defined as balanced surveillance systems composed of firms' structures, processes, and regulations that assert accountability and transparency to all stakeholders and investors while being socially accountable in all business operations (Solomon, 2020). Indeed, setting up an effective corporate governance mechanism on the board is considered to allow firms to perform more efficiently, improve capital access, ameliorate related risks, and secure existing stakeholders (Moussa et al., 2021; Muhammad et al., 2022). Correspondingly, the implication of robust corporate governance systems impacts firm performance and maintains sustainable economic growth (Albitar et al., 2023).

In this regard, environmental governance has garnered broad attention from academics, including social scientists, environmental scientists, policymakers, and practitioners in recent years (Rodrigue et al., 2013). It evolved as a more modern lens, extending traditional corporate governance's scope into directors' fiduciary responsibilities to stakeholders and the environment (Fisher et al., 2021). Corporate governance is the system by which companies are directed and controlled and is one of the most important factors in a company's success or failure. It refers to the role of a board of directors who are responsible for the governance of their organizations (Rodrigue et al., 2013).

As pointed out by Gibassier and Schaltegger (2015), firms and regulators are requested to consider environmental governance and related reporting with the same importance as financial reporting to achieve proper accountability and transparency for stakeholders. Environmental governance has been defined and conceptualized as a "set of regulatory processes, mechanisms, and organizations through which political actors influence environmental actions and outcomes" (Fisher et al., 2021). It encompasses the rules, practices, policies, and institutions that form how organizations interact with the environment and address environmental priorities (Moussa et al., 2021). From a stakeholder's perspective, environmental governance requires being accountable for their influence on society and stakeholders; boards, on the other hand, recognize their responsibilities to various stakeholders and their requirements and expectations. Therefore, firms should be more responsive to their stakeholders' expectations, which can be presented by environmental performance, and report positive results to their key stakeholders (Clarkson et al., 2008). As a result, environmental governance procedures, which are dedicated specifically to environmental oversight, provide boards with a framework for meeting stakeholder expectations regarding their environmental performance (Rodrigue et al., 2013).

However, there is a growing debate in the literature about how to measure corporate environmental performance. Given the wide range of available instruments and the lack of an operational definition, the measurement becomes complex. Like many other phenomena in organizational research, environmental performance cannot be directly observed and is considered as a construct (Trumpp et al., 2015). This means that the construct is connected to observable reality through indicators or measures, which are visible manifestations or aspects of a concept. One common approach to understanding a construct is to examine how it has been defined in the literature (Lisi, 2015).

Although the emerging stream of research discusses performance measurements in the environmental context, few studies have introduced a specific and comprehensive definition of environmental performance. This is primarily due to a lack of a unified and accepted definition of environmental performance and its operationalization (Asiaei et al., 2021; Trumpp et al., 2015). In this respect, the literature offered a number of definitions of environmental performance from different perspectives and contexts. For instance, some studies refer to the definition introduced by environmental organizations such as the International Organization for Standardization (ISO) 14031, which describes corporate environmental performance as a "measurable representation of the condition or status of operations, management, or conditions that provides information about an organization's performance related to the management of environmental aspects" (ISO, 2013). According to Trumpp et al. (2015), this definition is considered encompassing, parsimonious, and consensual since it captures the essential aspects of the environmental effects of management activities as well as these activities themselves. Juxtaposed with the academic perspectives and ISO 14031, the authors differentiate between two environmental performance pillars: operational performance and management performance. The first is mostly quantitative (i.e., inputs and outputs, regulatory compliance, and other environmental information related to product and service performance), but the latter captures the qualitative (i.e., policy, objectives, process, organizational structure, and monitoring).

In this study, we borrowed largely from the definition of Judge and Douglas (1998), who defined environmental performance as "a firm's effectiveness in meeting and exceeding society's expectations with respect to concerns for the natural environment." The latter definition was chosen as it supports the focus on both environmental impacts and a social dimension that considers the harmonious connection between society and external green stakeholders (Lisi, 2015).

Empirical studies on the link between environmental governance and environmental performance have had inclusive results (Bui et al., 2020; Zhu et al., 2021). For example, Berrone et al., (2010) found that environmental governance is negatively associated with corporate environmental performance. However, Rodrigue et al. (2013) found that environmental governance mechanisms do not influence environmental performance. They posit that environmental governance mechanisms serve mostly as a symbolic tool for managing stakeholder perceptions of environmental management and have a minor effect without making substantial changes to their operations. This is echoed by Haque (2017), who finds that while some mechanisms of corporate governance are linked to environmental performance based on processes (such as the implementation of carbon mitigation measures), other mechanisms are not linked to environmental performance based on outcomes (carbon emissions). In contrast, Zhu et al. (2021) suggested that environmental governance is a preliminary and imperative stage for more sustainable economic growth and environmental performance as a whole through lowering emissions while maintaining a predetermined production. Similarly, Bui et al. (2020) found that environmental governance mechanisms have positive associations with corporate environmental performance. The author's findings emphasized the strong integration of climate change issues in governance over traditional governance (such as board diversity, independence, duality, and size) in reflecting firms' commitments toward sustainability issues or providing more transparent reporting on environmental performance.

More specifically, environmental performance and governance are more aligned under the higher compliance of environment-related governance mechanisms (Bui et al., 2020). This is because firms under effective environmental governance strive to fulfill stakeholders' environmental expectations and address environmental performance issues (Shen & Chen, 2021). In contrast, under weak environmental governance, which may be symbolic rather than substantive compliance, firms employ these potentially symbolic practices to send environmental concern signals that do not translate into an improvement in environmental performance (Rodrigue et al., 2013). Accordingly, once stakeholders' perceptions have been managed appropriately and misled, they set aside their environmental expectations and create a false impression for their stakeholders about their actual environmental performance. Likewise, in an effort to preserve firms' legitimacy, boards may utilize symbolic environmental governance to offset management's proclivity for hiding information to conceal poor environmental performance and avoid accountability (de Villiers et al., 2022). Based on this perspective, we conjecture a positive association between environmental governance and corporate environmental performance. Thus, we formulate the following hypotheses:

H1: Environmental governance has a positive correlation with environmental performance.

4.1.2 Environmental Management Accounting and Environmental Performance

EMA is known as the management of non-financial and financial information within organizations to assess the impact of decisions aimed at advancing environmental performance on the financial well-being at the corporate level (Latan et al., 2018). From an environmental accounting perspective, EMA has been implemented primarily to regulate the utilization of natural resources, energy, and waste while also facilitating the identification of environment-related costs (Hanif et al., 2023). Moreover, EMA is positioned as a key driver of competitive advantage due to its broader scope compared to traditional management accounting practices, encompassing both monetary and physical dimensions (IFAC, 2005). It encompasses various resources, planning activities, and processes aimed at developing, implementing, evaluating, and sustaining environmental policies (Chaudhry & Amir, 2020), incorporating financial, physical, and non-financial considerations (Christ & Burritt, 2013). EMA facilitates strategic planning, control, and decision-making, particularly in the pursuit of environmental objectives (Tashakor et al., 2019) and when diverse environmental activities are involved. Indeed, EMA can also be considered as a decision-making framework to perform concrete and corrective actions when firms address environmental issues. In this regard, EMA integrates environmental information, including physical and monetary information on corporate activities, to guide managerial decisions in various green decision settings (Asiri et al., 2020). This information offered by EMA leads to achievement indicators for corporate environmental performance (Latan et al., 2018). Specifically, EMA can help firms meet environmental responsibility by identifying, assembling, utilizing, and evaluating the required information to make better decisions about their environmental strategy and performance (Chaudhry & Amir, 2020).

However, many organizations overlook environmental concerns in their accounting practices, as the conventional accounting approach is detrimental as it can adversely affect stakeholders (Hanif et al., 2023). When firms prioritize profit maximization over environmentally sustainable practices, they may encounter substantial financial consequences in the future, owing to the contemporary emphasis on environmental sustainability (Boakye et al., 2021). Stakeholders exert notable pressure on corporations to enhance their environmental performance, prompting businesses to engage in diverse initiatives aimed at actively contributing to environmental preservation (Hanif et al., 2023). Aligned with conventional management accounting practices, EMA encompasses both prospective analysis and retrospective record-keeping (Drury, 2013). Specifically, EMA can promote the identification of emerging threats and opportunities, support environmental decision-making and managerial coordination, promote alignment with organizational goals and values, and facilitate learning (Appannan et al., 2023).

Several research studies emphasize the importance of EMA in achieving environmental sustainability and suggest that organizations can gain a competitive advantage in the market by enhancing their environmental performance through the proper implementation of EMA (Sands & Lee, 2015). Through the adoption of EMA systems, organizations can both encourage environmental quality and gain financial, economic, and environmental benefits, especially when environmental considerations are integrated into financial reporting practices, i.e., corporate annual reports (Gunarathne & Lee, 2015). EMA's potential to enhance corporate environmental performance is also emphasized by Chaudhry and Amir (2020), who argue that EMA enables businesses to gain deeper insights into the dynamics of their environmental management systems, thus enabling more informed and efficient environmental-related decision-making. Furthermore, EMA is associated with enhanced production process efficiency, reduced material waste (Qian et al., 2018), and mitigating the environmental impact of firms' activities by identifying environmental costs and liabilities (Asiaei et al., 2021). In addition, EMA has different tools to help managers search for relevant information to inform them of different factors associated with the industry's financial and environmental performance.

Advocates emphasize how EMA provides firms with a platform to evaluate their current environmental standing, identify critical environmental concerns, and raise green economic opportunities associated with resource utilization, ultimately contributing to overall firm performance improvement (Gerged et al., 2024). Likewise, they have demonstrated that EMA tools, such as Material Flow Cost Accounting (MFCA), Activity-Based Costing (ABC), or Life-Cycle Assessment (LCA), have the potential to foster employee engagement with environmentally sustainable practices and improve organizational performance (Qian et al., 2018). Accordingly, it is suggested that adopting EMA can assist an organization by giving useful information on its operational activities, particularly concerning the environment, thus, in turn, stimulating corporate environmental performance. Based on the preceding considerations, the following hypothesis is proposed:

H2: Environmental management accounting has a positive correlation with environmental performance.

4.1.3 Environmental Governance, Environmental Management Accounting, and Environmental Performance

In this section, we predict that the environmental governance mechanisms, directly and indirectly, affect environmental performance through EMA. Both environmental governance and EMA have an effect on environmental performance, as illustrated in the previous sections. In this study, we propose that some of the contradictory findings regarding the association between environmental governance and environmental performance can be interpreted through the EMA mediating or moderating effect.

Theoretically, the natural resource-based view (NRBV) and stakeholders' theories have provided a framework for investigating the relationship between environmental governance and environmental performance as mediated by EMA. Specifically, NRBV argues that sustainable competitive advantages and the ability to create profits can be obtained through merging valuable organizational resources that are difficult to imitate or substitute and capabilities (Hart, 1995). Furthermore, the specific capabilities of the organization can save costs, optimize operations, enhance product quality, differentiate products, increase staff morale, and eventually manage the reputation and image, which is what the stakeholder theory is predominately concerned with. Evidence shows that good performance (environmental and financial) reflects strong organizational and management capabilities (Asiri et al., 2020; Hartmann & Vachon, 2018). In addition, the latter associations can be stronger under good governance structures and managerial capabilities, enabling environmentally friendly economic activities and leading to more robust environmental performance (Bui et al., 2020).

Given the broader developments in the realm of governance and environmental accounting research literature, the significance of the board's structure and process role in bolstering environmental performance in recent years has been acknowledged. For instance, Hillman and Dalziel (2003) suggest that the board has two main functions, namely (1) to monitor management to ensure that it is acting in the best interests of stakeholders and (2) to facilitate access to information and other critical resources, including environmental resources, thereby inducing environmental performance. In this regard, the recognized role of the environmental governance mechanisms that emanate from the board is to monitor, which may constrain any wrong treatments that are generally concerned with the implications of accounting choices (Ghosh & Wolf, 2021). Thus, when boards need to report their firms' environmental performance, management will be concerned about meeting this need. Likewise, the environmental governance mechanisms reflect a board's willingness to prevent litigation, regulatory enforcement costs, and reputational damage over the long term (Moussa et al., 2021). de Villiers et al. (2011), provide evidence that corporate governance characteristics represent the role of the board's monitoring and resource provision in enhancing corporate environmental performance. In this sense, robust governance mechanisms seek to improve environmental management activities within the firm by monitoring managerial decisions and control systems combined with providing necessary resources (Rodrigue et al., 2013).

Relatedly, Clarkson et al. (2008) provide empirical evidence that the existence of the EMA facilitates recognition and understanding of the necessity of environmental information, such as environmental cost, and consequently, their appropriate reporting to fulfill stakeholders' expectations. EMA is a system that provides information on physical or monetary terms to support decision-makers in achieving the firm objectives while paving the way for sustainable business (Bartolomeo et al., 2000). In this regard, firms with environmental commitment seek to distinguish themselves from their rivals by indicating to stakeholders their superior environmental performance; thereby, EMA has the potential to develop into a valuable capability, conferring a competitive advantage (Clarkson et al., 2008). The study determines that environmental governance and EMA have a positive correlation with improved environmental performance. Additionally, when considering investments for sustainable development, decisions regarding investment in EMA systems necessitate approval from the board. This is because the board has a duty and responsibility to consider the interests of not only shareholders but also other stakeholders who may be impacted by the firm's activities (Rodrigue et al., 2013). Hence, there is a positive relationship between environmental governance mechanisms and the presence of EMA systems. This suggests that one of the responsibilities of boards, through environmental governance mechanisms, should be to guarantee the effectiveness of EMA systems. Consequently, in theory, the role of EMA in connecting environmental governance and environmental performance has significant potential as a mediating factor.

Empirically, the association between environmental governance and EMA can affect environmental governance's relationship with other dimensions of operations performance, including underlying corporate environmental performance. For instance, Zeiler (2004) investigates the relationship between governance characteristics, board actions/decisions, and firm CSR performance and finds that the characteristics-performance link is mediated by board actions/decisions. Similarly, Orazalin (2020) examines the mediation effect of sustainability practices on the association between the presence of a board sustainability committee as an environmental governance mechanism and the likelihood of better corporate environmental performance and provides evidence of a mediation effect. In a recent study, Ghosh and Wolf (2021) explored how environmental accounting practices impact hybrid governance forms and performance. They argue that integrating environmental accounting into governance routines creates new opportunities for adaptation and improvement, ultimately influencing environmental and economic performance. Similarly, Nkundabanyanga and Muramuzi (2021) investigated the connection between EMA and board role performance (BRP) on the environmental performance of manufacturing companies. Their findings suggest that EMA mediates the relationship between BRP and corporate environmental performance. Therefore, based on the theoretical framework and the discussion presented, it is assumed that EMA can mediate the relationship between environmental governance and environmental performance.

At the same time, EMA can play a moderating role in environmental governance mechanisms and environmental performance nexus. Scholars widely suggest that the governance mechanisms related to environmental issues employed by boards direct organizational activities toward tangible changes in actions to improve environmental performance, likely achievable through the robust adoption of EMA (Latan et al., 2018; Moussa et al., 2021). In that context, boards can consider EMA as the primary control tool that fulfills the strategic organizational needs for sustainable development by providing the management with information related to monetary and unmonetized soft aspects (Latan et al., 2018). In this respect, EMA can play a significant role in facilitating interdependence and fostering communication within the organizational structure; it is rational to believe it would be carried out effectively when developing EMA systems that may be contingent on inter-functional communication (Bartolomeo et al., 2000).

EMA is designed to provide decision-makers with information that addresses their concerns and evaluates the performance of the environmental management process in relation to the organizational objectives. It is hypothesized that a higher commitment to EMA implementation by a company will have a more significant impact in supporting environmental governance mechanisms and creating an appropriate control environment, leading to a better understanding of the information needs related to environmental performance. Conversely, low levels of EMA implementation in a firm may result in decision-makers and policymakers lacking measurable information on environmental impact, governance, stakeholder communication, and organizational systems, which are important in illustrating the interaction between management and the environment (Wang et al., 2018). In this scenario, when there is low communication and coordination among members of a company, the hidden potential within the organization, like reduced material and energy use and improved waste management, remains untapped. Therefore, EMA can be seen as the main tool for organizational management control systems. It supports environmental governance and creates a suitable control environment that encourages environmental performance.

As a result, the gap between environmental governance and corporate environmental performance is likely to decrease when EMA is effectively incorporated. This is due to the influence of EMA as a significant control factor on the connection between environmental governance and environmental performance. Specifically, we anticipate that environmental governance will have a positive impact on environmental performance when firms extensively implement EMA through a substantive approach. Therefore, the moderating effect of EMA that strengthens the relationship between environmental governance mechanisms and corporate environmental performance is considered undeniable. Based on these arguments, we suggest that EMA can mediate or moderate the relationship between environmental governance and environmental performance. Consequently, the following hypotheses are proposed:

H3(a): Environmental management accounting mediates the relationship between environmental governance and environmental performance.

H3(b): Environmental management accounting moderates the relationship between environmental governance and environmental performance.

4.2 Research Methodology

4.2.1 The Italian Context

The European Commission has issued Directive 2014/95/EU, which aims to rebuild trust with investors and consumers. This directive requires certain large businesses and groups to disclose non-financial reporting information, specifically related to sustainable development, environmental and social matters, anti-corruption efforts, human rights, and boardroom diversity (Commission, 2014). Latterly, the NFRD has been incorporated into Italian law by Legislative Decree 254/2016, particularly with respect to extra elements such as undertaking business models, policies, and the impact of the activities in relation to social and environmental issues. In consonance with these EU rules, public-interest entities (PIEs) are required to disclose their non-financial information (NFI) regularly, commencing on 1st January 2017 and onwards.[1] Moreover, the legislative changes demonstrate the increased expectations on businesses to disclose non-financial performance and identify sustainability risks as demanded by stakeholders (Clementino & Perkins, 2021). As a result,

[1] Large undertakings (PIEs and firms with more than 500 employees) are subject to the directive when they meet the following criteria: (1) Total net sales and service revenues: € 40 million; (2) Total assets: € 20 million.

these regulations promote growth and enhance investor and consumer confidence (Commission, 2014). We will consider this analysis after the implementation of the aforementioned legislative decree.

We have chosen Italy as it is committed to the environment and society, with highly stringent regulations to meet the needs of the relevant stakeholders (Veltri & Ferraro, 2018). However, in early 2020, and precisely during the first quarter of the same year, Italy faced the threat of economic downturns due to the coronavirus (COVID-19) outbreak. This viral epidemic was first identified in China, not limited to medical aspects, but has resulted in substantial global sociological, psychological, and economic repercussions (Guo et al., 2020). Italy has the third-highest number of coronavirus cases, following the United States and Spain, which have enforced an extreme quarantine measure and total lockdowns after the immersing spike in cases. As a result, investors became increasingly worried about corporate debt and liquidity, indicating widespread concerns that the health crisis may evolve into a financial crisis. These effects can be particularly severe for some sectors, such as tourism and hospitality. The COVID-19 global pandemic undoubtedly creates a challenging environment for all facets of the economy in terms of tighter financial limitations, and unfavorable economic conditions hurt corporate environmental performance, lowering green investments and hence potentially slowing the shift to a low-carbon economy (Guérin & Suntheim, 2021). In response to these serious challenges, numerous research studies have been conducted (Guérin & Suntheim, 2021; Kang et al., 2021). The prevailing research suggests a growing emphasis on the sustainable use of resources and the resilience of organizations. Despite the potential long-term impact of the COVID-19 pandemic due to the tremendous uniqueness of this phenomenon on firms' actual environmental performance, there have been few analyses into the aggregate impact of the COVID-19 crisis on corporate environmental performance and green investments to support the transition to a low-carbon economy (Guérin & Suntheim, 2021). This prospect opens several avenues for future research into the relatively unexplored area of environmental reporting.

4.2.2 *Sample and Data Collection*

This research study uses a dataset of FTSE 100 firms that are listed on the Italian Stock Exchange as of December 31, 2018, to empirically examine the role of EMA in the relationship between environmental governance and environmental performance. According to the Borsa Italiana website, we can categorize the listed firms into three main Italian stock indices based on market value: The FTSE MIB is the primary benchmark index, consisting of the 40 most-traded and highly liquid stock classes on the exchange. The FTSE MIB index includes firms that represent roughly 80 percent of the domestic market capitalization. The FTSE Italia Mid Cap index (market capitalization between \$2 and \$10 billion) represents the top 60 most liquid and highest-capitalized firms outside the FTSE MIB index. Lastly, the FTSE Italia Small Cap index (FTITSC) or Star issuers (capitalization of less than $2 billion) comprises shares of the remaining small firms that are not included in the FTSE MIB and FTSE Italia Mid Cap indexes.

The selection of FTSE is justified by several considerations. FTSE firms can be esteemed as leading organizations in disclosing Sustainable Development Goals and practices and are likely to invest a lot of time and resources in reporting their social and environmental performance data (Veltri & Ferraro, 2018). Moreover, they are typically transparent, genuine, and proactive, which makes public information more convenient for investors to identify and assess them, as they are more responsive to the needs and expectations of the global community (Veltri & Ferraro, 2018). It is also worth noting that FTSE firms are cross-listing, which can be seen as a determinant of the quality of financial and non-financial information that reflects compliance with international disclosure requirements toward promoting positivism and capabilities to sustainable practices and green activities (Clementino & Perkins, 2021). This would contribute to safeguarding and extending the number of firm stakeholders, boost non-financial aspects, and develop the capabilities and skills that are useful for enhancing environmental performance (Veltri & Ferraro, 2018). As a result, the sustainability committee is more frequent in FTSE firms than in similar firms that do not cross-list. Lastly, FTSE has been extensively used in recent empirical studies built upon multi-country samples (Clementino & Perkins, 2021) and the Italian context as well (Veltri & Ferraro, 2018).

Among firms in the initial sample, we exclude firms with missing environmental and governance data. We then exclude duplicated firms and firms with missing financial or economic information for control variables. In addition, financial firms have been excluded. This study does not analyze financial corporations such as commercial banks and insurance firms for their specific governance and regulatory rules, as the information given by the annual reports of financial institutions is not comparable with the forms of businesses. In addition, these firms are also not highly involved in industrial pollution and energy consumption (Moussa et al., 2021).

In light of the preceding criteria, our final sample is 70 Italian firms representing 350 firm-year observations. We collected data from three main sources: The environmental data are drawn from the Thomson Reuters Refinitiv Eikon database. Financial and control data are extracted from the Aida Database developed by Bureau van Dijk. In addition, supplementary information from the Italian Stock Exchange website contains the official data of the listed publicly traded firms. The samples are heterogeneous as they are subdivided into ten industry sectors, as shown in the complete analyzed firms in Table 4.1. Nevertheless, the data from 5 consecutive years covering the period from 2017 until 2021, since Italy has witnessed unprecedented economic challenges during this period, make the Italian case worth examining.

Table 4.1 Sample distribution by industry

S. No	Industry	No. of Firms	No of firm observations	Frequency (%)
1	Energy and natural resources	4	20	6
2	Health care	4	20	6
3	Information technology	2	10	3
4	Telecommunications services	3	15	4
5	Utilities	13	65	19
6	Consumer staples	5	25	7
7	Consumer discretionary	17	85	24
8	Manufacturing and construction	2	10	3
9	Basic material	2	10	3
10	Industrials	18	90	26
Total		70	350	100

4.2.3 Variables Measurement

We used various measures to assess the main study variables, drawing from measures used in previous studies. However, Dragomir (2018) suggests that when researchers try to measure a multifaceted concept, they encounter difficulties because each researcher chooses a different measure for the same concept. For example, the methods used to gauge corporate environmental performance in academic research vary depending on the research objectives, scopes, and data availability (Zhang & Wellalage, 2022). Buntaine (2011) emphasizes that environmental performance is linked to environmental goals and efforts to reduce environmental impact and can be measured using output-based and input-based performance measures. Recently, the authors collected quantitative data on corporate environmental performance by analyzing corporate reports, annual reports, sustainability reports, websites, and other public disclosures, either through content analysis methods or surveys distributed to environmental managers of the sampled firms.

Some authors also conduct fieldwork and interviews with environmental managers to collect data from firms without intermediaries. In addition, third-party environmental databases hold detailed data spanning numerous facilities and years (de Villiers et al., 2022). Their reliability hinges on whether submitted data are cross-validated, independently certified, or otherwise create demand to ascertain the reported statements. Third-party agents provide large listed firms with the list of firms with substantial ESG performance, such as environmental or ESG scores reported in the KLD and Refinitiv databases (Zhang & Wellalage, 2022). Scoring systems vary, with some emphasizing reliability and others construct validity. Nonetheless, all rating providers aim to assure users of product reliability, uniformity, comprehensiveness, and relevance. Access to specific databases, regardless of data collection methods, remains crucial.

The commonly used Kinder, Lydenberg, Domini Research and Analytics (KLD) ratings, developed by RiskMetrics (currently known as MSCI ESG STATS), are criticized for their poor reliability due to broad indicators and inadequate sensitivity in scoring positive and negative aspects (Bui et al., 2020). Despite these shortcomings, KLD ratings are extensively employed in research despite their methodological flaws and limited variability (Cho et al., 2010; Michelon et al., 2020). Other tools like the Thomson Reuters Refinitiv Eikon database offer better construct validity and methodological transparency, providing a global corporate environmental performance score encompassing a broader range of indicators that enhance its construct validity. The database is used by academics interested in sustainability-related themes, although it was originally developed for professional use (Trumpp et al., 2015). Then, the Refinitiv database is a leading global platform that provides a measurement approach to environmental performance that is objective, relevant, consistent, systematic, and auditable data about the three pillars of environmental, social, and corporate governance (ESG) information, relying on more than 250 firm sustainability performance indicators (Moussa et al., 2021). As Trumpp et al. (2015) point out, Refinitiv is the only publicly available database offering non-aggregated data for EOP and EMP aspects of corporate environmental performance. Specifically, the underlying measures express how effectively a business employs best management practices to manage environmental risks and seize environmental opportunities. While the Refinitiv database stands out for its methodological transparency, its proprietary nature restricts researchers' control. Future developments for the database are anticipated to enhance understanding of its scoring system and expand the indicators list for increased credibility and data reliability (Dragomir, 2018). Appendix A represents the measure of variables.

Corporate Environmental Performance

Environmental performance is defined as "a firm's effectiveness in meeting and exceeding society's expectations with respect to concerns for the natural environment" (Judge & Douglas, 1998). Environmental performance encompasses how effectively a firm manages resources, energy, and water, designing an eco-efficient range of products and services, and pollution abatement (Lisi, 2015). Based on the above multidimensional insights, we extracted the aggregated environmental pillar score from the Thomson Reuters Refinitiv Eikon database to measure corporate environmental performance. The environmental score from the Refinitiv database has increasingly been validated in the literature and is widely used in recent studies (Albitar et al., 2023; Haque, 2017; Qiu et al., 2016), considering its extensiveness and transparency. This database is used by academics interested in sustainability-related themes, although it was originally developed for professional use (Trumpp et al., 2015). The Refinitiv is a global database that offers a comprehensive platform that provides objective, relevant, systematic measures regarding the three pillars of environmental, social, and governance (ESG), relying on more than 250 firm sustainability performance indicators (Moussa et al., 2021). In addition, it expresses how effectively a business employs best management practices to manage environmental risks and seize environmental opportunities (Hartmann & Vachon, 2018). In accordance with Refinitiv, environmental performance is measured based on roughly equal-weighted ratings covering three categories: carbon emission reduction, environmental resource use, and product innovation. The environmental score reflects firms' performance and capacity to reduce material and energy use, improve water recycling, lower carbon emissions, and create market opportunities through environmental innovation activities (de Villiers et al., 2022). The aggregated scores lie between 0 and 100%; the higher the score, the better the corporate environmental performance is likely to be.

Environmental Governance

We use the existence of sustainability assurance, sustainability committee, emission mitigation target horizon, and GRI guidelines adoption as the basis of our combined measure of environmental governance strength (Bui et al., 2020; Liao et al., 2015; Moussa et al., 2021). Accordingly, we initially examine whether the firm publishes sustainability reports in accordance with Global Reporting Initiative (GRI) guidelines. The GRI guidelines are the most widely implemented in any firm that seeks a comprehensive approach to measure and disclose information on their environmental performance to a wide range of stakeholders and business operations (Clementino & Perkins, 2021). It provides organizations with a set of guidelines to measure and disclose their sustainability performance information, which helps them comprehend and communicate their organizational impact on the environment (GRI, 2002). Firms that adopt the GRI are more likely to implement environmentally friendly management practices and are inclined to provide transparent and comprehensive information to their stakeholders on their environmental performance than those that do not (Michelon et al., 2015). GRI compliance is quantified in terms of the percentage of organizations that adhere to the GRI's sustainability reporting guidelines.

We further examine whether the presence of the sustainability committee (B_SC) impacts environmental performance. The impact of establishing a sustainability committee on environmental performance is amidst ongoing debate in the literature. For instance, prior studies contend that sustainability committees' presence positively contributes to corporate environmental performance (de Villiers et al., 2022; Liao et al., 2015; Muhammad & Migliori, 2023). Similarly, Haque (2017) argues that sustainability committees play a fundamental role in tracking firms' social and environmental commitments. Along similar lines, Liao et al. (2015) postulate that the board with the sustainability committee shows a higher tendency to be environmentally transparent. In contrast, Berrone and Gomez-Mejia (2009) found no association between the environmental committee's presence and environmental performance based on their analysis of a sample of 469 US firms. Therefore, having a well-structured sustainability committee that is responsible for the CSR strategy and performance, which in turn, facilitates the development of a competitive advantage for the business (Liao et al., 2015). Further, we examine the time horizon of climate change risk targets on environmental reporting (CERT). Setting the time horizon of risk information and risk strategy can play a vital role in controlling environmental pollution and achieving emissions reductions by providing economic incentives (Hartmann & Vachon, 2018).

Given the importance of sustainability reporting, some firms are taking further steps that are most likely to enhance the integrity and reliability of published sustainability reports by adopting sustainability assurance activities (Moussa et al., 2021). Although this additional scrutiny associated with assurance adoption can substantially incur additional costs to the firms, they can yield a significant effect by signaling their environmental performance to key stakeholders, which leads to maintaining credibility and ensuring accountability of the disclosed reports' contents (Clarkson et al., 2008). Therefore, we examine whether firms appoint external sustainability audits (SEA) to ascertain their sustainability reports by having external audit statements for their environmental data. Accordingly, we sum these components to obtain a collective score for environmental governance ranging from 0 to 7.

Environmental Management Accounting

EMA is a technique to promote and use financial and non-financial information to support decision-makers in achieving the firm objectives while paving the way for sustainable business in the form of green or environmentally friendly activities (Bartolomeo et al., 2000). In this regard, EMA represents the activities undertaken by firms to enhance their environmental and economic performance and contribute to sustainable business development (Latan et al., 2018). However, some EMA research has suggested that the potentially high costs of adopting EMA could be a challenge or barrier to some firms, particularly for those not well-endowed in resources (Brooks & Oikonomou, 2018). In addition, employing a proper environmental management control system (such as EMA) necessitates firms investing heavily in accounting staff training, research and development, and the acquisition of environmental technologies (Asiri et al., 2020). Our construct, therefore, measures the main aspects of EMA systems that compile and analyze monetary and physical aspects to identify the EMA implementation. In addition, we chose indicators that can be applied to firms from several industry sectors and demonstrate concrete initiatives and actions to reduce ecosystem degradation. Following prior studies (Bartolomeo et al., 2000; Chaudhry & Amir, 2020; Gunarathne et al., 2021; Hartmann & Vachon, 2018; Latan et al., 2018; Lisi, 2015), we include the following components to obtain a composite score for EMA.

First, we check the existence of the environmental management team (EM_Team), which performs the functions that bring together accounting and environmental staff to meet environmental objectives. This emphasizes the logical link between accounting and environmental management functions, including coordinating accounting, environmental management, and operational data (Bartolomeo et al., 2000). An important means to obtain financial literacy among environmental managers and enlighten environmental awareness among accounting staff toward environmental improvement (Asiri et al., 2020). Then, we checked whether the firm engages in emission trading initiatives (ET) by providing economic incentives to reduce contaminants' emissions (Naranjo Tuesta et al., 2021), which affects physical inputs and outputs. Under a regulatory context such as the European emissions trading scheme, firms are required to take action towards emission reductions or bear additional allowances, which is more costly in comparison to when firms take environmental actions and engage in environmental protection programs (Hartmann & Vachon, 2018).

In addition, we also check whether the firm accounting system records all environmental expenditures (EEI), such as materials, energy, water, wastes (i.e., disposal, treatment, sanitation, and clean-up), and emissions (Wang et al., 2018). We also checked whether the firm designed a product line or service to positively affect the environment and/or whether the firm evaluated projects financially (EP) appertaining to environmental or biodiversity risks based on project financing data (Wang et al., 2018).

Furthermore, consistent with the work of (Gomez-Conde et al., 2019), we outline the effect of environmental management training (EMT). Firms investing in employee and management training empower managers and accounting staff with new capabilities to recognize environmental issues and identify novel environmentally friendly solutions. This encourages cross-fertilization of knowledge and ideas when deviations from the environmental process between environmental management and management accounting functions occur (Bartolomeo et al., 2000).

We follow the approach of prior studies (de Villiers & van Staden, 2011; Naranjo Tuesta et al., 2021) to identify whether the aspects related to EMA implementation systems are linked with positive environmental returns against those firms that have not implemented one. Such soft information can affect profitability and financial status and provide regulatory-based incentives to implement these systems (Gunarathne et al., 2021). Thus, we check whether the firms received awards for their socio-environmental performance (CSR_AW). Based on a review of 53 scientific papers examining a total of 182,926 firms, Erauskin-Tolosa et al. (2020) suggest that firms obtaining sustainability awards, such as Eco-Management and Audit Scheme (EMAS), have a positive effect on their environmental performance. Lastly, a proxy measure, such as an environmental management system certificate (CERTIFICATE), was employed in our study to check whether the firm holds an ISO 14001 certification (Lisi, 2015). The variable contains information about companies that have received an environmental certification, such as ISO 14001. This reflects whether the existence of a management control system affects an organization's performance as a tool for achieving its strategic objectives compared to firms that have not adopted one (Erauskin-Tolosa et al., 2020). A dichotomous variable is utilized to measure each component, giving the value 1 if the firm takes the corresponding item and 0 otherwise. Therefore, the construct is calculated as the collective score of the variable components of 7 indicators, ranging between 0 and 7.

Control Variables

The study controls for binary-specific characteristics and governance mechanisms that may impact environmental performance, which varies according to the firm's financial conditions and the effects of the industry. In line with prior studies, we include a number of variables representing corporate variables that may influence the extent of corporate environmental performance (Liao et al., 2015; Moussa et al., 2021). These include board size (BS), measured by the number of board directors. Independent board directors measure board independence (BI) as a percentage. Executive duality (CEO_D) is a dummy variable, which indicates that the board chairman is also the chief executive officer (CEO) given the value 1; 0 otherwise. Lastly, we study the impacts of gender diversity on environmental performance. Liao et al. (2015) reported a significant positive association between gender diversity and environmental performance. For this study, gender diversity (B_GD) is expressed in women directors' percentages on the board (Liao et al., 2015).

We further control for industry effects. Prior research indicates that firms in environmentally sensitive sectors exhibited higher environmental performance due to the intensifying public and stakeholder pressures to represent their interests fully (Bui et al., 2020; Michelon et al., 2015). The environmentally sensitive industry (ESI) variable is a dummy variable measured as follows: 1 if a firm operates in the environmentally sensitive industry and 0 otherwise. According to Asiri et al. (2020), firms that operate in highly environmentally sensitive sectors are associated with strict environmental legislation, which requires including the environmental impacts of their activities in the annual reports provided to government regulators or regional authorities. We also include the environmental controversies sensitivity (ECS) score, as firms in highly environmentally sensitive industries are more exposed to media's spotlights and stakeholder visibility (Moussa et al., 2021). Such firms are more likely to exhibit a higher environmental performance because they tend not to infringe on environmental regulation and are less likely to be embroiled in environmental controversies (Bui et al., 2020).

Lastly, we control for variables representing firm-specific characteristics. These include firm size (FS), measured as the natural logarithm of each total firm's assets (Michelon et al., 2015). However, we tested this variable as large-sized firms tend to be accompanied by more resources (e.g., total assets) aligned with environmental pollution practices (Liao et al., 2015). On the other hand, larger firms pay more attention to environmental challenges due to regulatory pressure (Bui et al., 2020). Firm age (FA) was measured as a logarithm number of years since it was founded (Liao et al., 2015). Leverage and financial performance were employed to capture financial risk and resource availability. Financial leverage (FL) was determined as the ratio of long-term debts to total assets (Bui et al., 2020). Lastly, financial performance (FP) is proxied by the return on assets (Qian et al., 2018).

Research Models

In this study, ordinary least squares (OLS) regression is used to analyze the relationship among variables.[2] Generally, OLS regression is suitable for describing and validating our hypotheses and is consistent with prior research studies (Asiaei et al., 2023; Bui et al., 2020; Qian et al., 2018). To test our hypotheses and examine how environmental governance mechanisms affect environmental performance through EMA, we employed the following regression models based on the well-established line of research regarding the mediating and moderating effect (Baron & Kenny, 1986; Muhammad et al., 2022; Preacher & Hayes, 2008).

$$EP_{it} = \beta 0 + \beta_1 EG_{it} + \beta_2 \sum_i \text{control variables} + \varepsilon_{it} \tag{4.1}$$

$$\mathrm{ENV\_MA}_{it} = \beta 0 + \beta_1 \mathrm{EG}_{it} + \beta_2 \sum_i \text{control variables} + \varepsilon_{it} \tag{4.2}$$

$$\mathrm{EP}_{it} = \beta 0 + \beta_1 \mathrm{ENV\_MA}_{it} + \beta_2 \sum_i \text{control variables} + \varepsilon_{it} \tag{4.3}$$

$$\mathrm{EP}_{it} = \beta 0 + \beta_1 \mathrm{EG}_{it} + \beta_2 \mathrm{ENV\_MA}_{it} + \beta_3 \sum_i \text{control variables} + \varepsilon_{it} \tag{4.4}$$

$$\begin{aligned}\mathrm{EP}_{i} = {} & \beta 0 + \beta_1 \mathrm{EG}_{i} + \beta_2 \mathrm{ENV\_MA}_{i} + \left(\beta_3 \mathrm{EG}_{i} * \beta_2 \mathrm{ENV\_MA}_{i}\right) \\ & + \beta_4 \sum_i \text{control variables} + \varepsilon_{it}\end{aligned} \tag{4.5}$$

where EP_{it} denotes the environmental performance of firm *i* in time *t*, EG_{it} represents environmental governance of firm *i* in time *t*. ENV_MA_{it} is the environmental management accounting and ε_{it} is a specific error term. These variables are defined below in Appendix A.

4.2.4 Descriptive Statistics

The data in Table 4.2 reported the descriptive statistics of all study variables. As shown, the mean of environmental performance (EP) score is 56.73%, with a standard deviation of 24.50. These results are in line with the Yale Center for Environmental Law and Policy (YCELP) latest report on Italy's environmental

[2] In the absence of endogeneity issues within the model, ordinary least squares (OLS) regression is well-suited and can be conducted. However, when the endogeneity probability increases, the OLS estimators become biased (Blundell & Bond, 1998).

Table 4.2 Descriptive statistics

Variables	Obs	Mean	Std. Dev.	Min	Max
EP	350	56.733	24.503	0	98.91
EG	350	3.783	2.053	0	7
GRI	350	0.746	0.436	0	1
B SC	350	0.751	0.433	0	1
CERT	350	1.357	1.595	0	4
SA	350	0.929	0.258	0	1
ENV MA	350	3.451	2.079	0	7
EM team	350	0.546	0.503	0	1
ET	350	0.229	0.421	0	1
EEI	350	0.354	0.479	0	1
EP	350	0.554	0.498	0	1
EMT	350	0.706	0.456	0	1
CSR AW	350	0.366	0.482	0	1
CERTIFICATE	350	0.723	0.448	0	1
BS	350	10.991	2.698	6	23
BI	350	53.732	15.094	11.11	92.59
CEO D	350	0.831	0.375	0	1
BGD	350	35.8	6.581	12.5	57.14
ESI	350	0.529	0.5	0	1
ECS	350	89.37	26.427	3.31	100
FS	350	3.483	0.715	2.3	5.435
FA	350	57.58	41.453	2	184
FL	350	0.427	0.23	0	0.93
FP	350	6.813	7.626	−14.4	59.75

performance score.[3] The independent and control variables show that the mean of environmental governance (EG) is 3.783. The average adoption of GRI guidelines is 74.60% of the sampled firms when preparing sustainability reports. The sustainability committee (B_SC) appears to be a typical practice, as evidenced by the fact that, on average, 75.10% of the studied firms maintained a sustainability committee in the boardroom. Further, the Emission reduction target (CERT) has a mean of 1.357, representing a high proportion of firms with no emissions reduction target or stretching beyond 2025. Finally, the mean of sustainability external audit (SA) is around 93%, representing that most firms have external auditors (i.e., experts, academics, an external panel, or a research center) and provide external assurance statements for their sustainability data.

EMA (ENV_MA) scoring postulates a slightly similar mean value of 3.451. The mean of the environmental management team (EM_Team) is 54%, which exhibits that sampled firms with pro-environmental orientation and the link between the

[3] Italian environmental performance was ranked 16th out of 180 by YCELP (2022), with a score of 57.7%. https://epi.yale.edu/downloads/epi2022policymakerssummary.pdf

accounting and environmental management functions are slightly high. In contrast, the mean of CSR sustainability awards (CSR_AW) is 36.6%, which designates that firms received environmental awards or were assessed positively on their sustainability performance during the 5-year period. Lastly, we find that 72.30% of the sampled firms hold ISO 14001 certification as a considerable indicator for implementing environmental management systems. This indicates that the sampled firms may be more inclined to develop dynamic capabilities toward green economy opportunities and improve emission performance (Marrucci et al., 2022). With regards to corporate governance-specific variables, the sampled firms have 11 members on their boards, with a minimum of 6 and a maximum of 23. On average, independent board directors (BI) represent 53.73% of the board.

On the other hand, 81.3% of the CEOs of the sample firms are board members (CEO_D). The mean of board gender diversity (B_GD) is 35.8, which shows that at least three females are present in the boardroom. This results in consonance with Italian law no. 120/2011, which requires the public companies listed in the stock market to allotter 33% of board members for women slated by 2015. Concerning specific environmental variables, environmentally sensitive industry (ESI) shows that, on average, highly polluting industries are more likely to be inclined to provide additional environmental information to reduce potential sanctions and meet the investors' information needs (Ntim & Soobaroyen, 2013). In this regard, global investment management corporations prioritize climate-friendly governance at their portfolio firms. They anticipate that board members will develop long-term strategies to evaluate and minimize climate risk. For example, BlackRock (Angerio, 2020) identified 244 giant organizations that have insufficient actions to address climate issues and resolve their issues in the organizational structure. Blackrock admonished over 50 firms for engaging in 'unsustainable' practices and inaction on tackling global warming and climate change. Indeed, the effective implementation of political, legal, and economic support can play an effective role in the dialogue's implementation between science and society on a global scope. Lastly, the mean environmental controversies sensitivity (ECS) is 89.37%, indicating that the sampled firms are exposed to greater environmental controversy and adverse events reflected in global media.

4.2.5 Correlation Matrix

The correlation matrix between dependent, independent, and control variables is shown in Table 4.3. The Pearson correlation coefficients for environmental performance (EP) are statistically significant and positively related to environmental governance and environmental management accounting. It is well shown that most control variables positively and significantly correlate with environmental performance. The negative correlations are observed for environmental controversies sensitivity (ECS) and firm performance (FP). Furthermore, a high correlation level is detected for firm size (FS) at 0.568, environmental governance (EG) at 0.551,

Table 4.3 Correlation matrix

Variables	EP	EG	ENV_ MA	BS	BI	CEO_D	BGD	ESI	ECS	FS	FA	FL	FP
EP	1												
EG	0.551***	1											
ENV_ MA	0.550***	0.472***	1										
BS	0.316***	0.239***	0.134*	1									
BI	0.393***	0.375***	0.332***	0.211***	1								
CEO_D	0.220***	0.153**	0.175**	0.0779	0.146**	1							
BGD	0.0560	0.158**	0.0940	−0.0866	0.146**	0.0783	1						
ESI	0.241***	0.361***	0.266***	−0.0667	0.205***	0.140**	0.0236	1					
ECS	−0.379***	−0.456***	−0.299***	−0.0504	−0.398***	−0.0531	−0.0791	−0.165**	1				
FS	0.568***	0.642***	0.479***	0.310***	0.504***	0.0720	−0.0222	0.292***	−0.563***	1			
FA	0.159**	0.0887	0.125*	−0.0364	−0.0785	0.00170	−0.0738	0.0377	−0.0683	0.252***	1		
FL	0.286***	0.257***	0.254***	0.307***	0.324***	0.155**	0.0278	0.174**	−0.0554	0.297***	−0.0353	1	
FP	−0.217***	−0.152**	−0.0826	−0.121*	−0.140**	0.0859	−0.178***	−0.152**	0.130*	−0.339***	−0.148**	−0.228***	1
VIF	–	1.80	1.46	1.30	1.60	1.10	1.19	1.27	1.64	1.95	1.18	1.33	1.30
Obs	350	350	350	350	350	350	350	350	350	350	350	350	350

Note: All variables are defined in Appendix A. VIF signifies the variance inflation factor. Sig. level: * $p < 0.05$, ** $p < 0.01$, *** $p < 0.001$

followed by EMA practices (ENV_MA) at 0.550. Environmental controversies sensitivity (ECS) has the lowest association with environmental performance, with a correlation of −0.379.

4.2.6 Regression Results and Discussion

In this section, we present the main regression results of the multivariant ordinary least squares (OLS) regression test. All regressions contain the effects of year, firm, and industry. Table 4.4 illustrates the main effect of environmental governance mechanisms and EMA practices on corporate environmental performance (including the control variables). These regression results are reported in columns (1)–(3). Column 1 indicates the main effect of environmental governance on environmental performance to test hypothesis 1. Column 2 reports the regression results of the EMA on environmental governance mechanisms. Finally, column 3 shows the main effect of EMA on environmental performance to test hypothesis 2.

As shown in column 1, the main effect of environmental governance on environmental performance is positive and significant *at* ($\beta = 3.005$ $p < 0.01$). This denotes that firms with robust environmental governance mechanisms exhibit higher corporate environmental performance. This result supports Hypothesis 1. This result is consistent with the prior empirical findings of Bui et al. (2020), Michelon et al. (2015), and Moussa et al. (2021) who have found a positive influence of environmental governance mechanisms (such as sustainability committees, GRI guidelines, emission mitigation target horizon, and sustainability assurance) on corporate environmental performances. The results are compatible with the stakeholder theory assertion that firms adopt environmental governance mechanisms as an assertive tactic to manage stakeholder impressions of firm environmental performance and fulfill their information needs (Michelon et al., 2015). These posit that GRI guidelines, board sustainability Committee, environmental risk horizon, and sustainability assurance promote corporate environmental performance and seek congruence with stakeholders' perceptions.

The results in column 2 show that the environmental governance mechanisms have a positive and significant association with EMA practices at (β = 1.232 $p < 0.01$). This result indicates that the higher-level integration of climate change into governance through environmental-embedded governance mechanisms positively affects the implementation of accounting information systems such as EMA at the firm level (Qian et al., 2018). This perspective suggests that strong environmental governance motivates management through EMA to communicate environmental information more extensively, which can help increase trust when dealing with stakeholders and strengthen the firm's position further in the eyes of stakeholders (Gunarathne et al., 2021). This can also be attributed to the fact that management in firms with weak environmental governance enjoys considerable discretion; thereby, increasing environmental governance may restrict such discretion (Bui et al., 2020).

Table 4.4 Baseline regression results

Dependent variables →	EP	ENV_MA	EP
Independent variables ↓	(1)	(2)	(3)
EG	3.005***	1.232***	
	(0.558)	(0.167)	
ENV_MA			3.387***
			(0.482)
BS	0.508*	0.169*	0.368**
	(0.281)	(0.097)	(0.176)
CEO_D	1.050	0.447**	0.559
	(1.530)	(0.184)	(1.483)
BI	0.061	0.0151	0.079
	(0.078)	(0.009)	(0.076)
BGD	0.202	0.041***	0.085
	(0.123)	(0.015)	(0.121)
ECS	−0.007	0.000	−0.031
	(0.036)	(0.004)	(0.034)
ESI	3.373	−0.116	9.072**
	(4.014)	(0.484)	(3.667)
FS	4.985***	2.703*	2.679***
	(1.529)	(1.545)	(1.049)
FL	6.983	1.612**	3.368
	(5.767)	(0.695)	(5.627)
FA	0.082	0.023*	0.041
	(0.100)	(0.012)	(0.097)
FP	0.027	−0.003	0.043
	(0.124)	(0.015)	(0.120)
Year effects	Yes	Yes	Yes
Firm effects	Yes	Yes	Yes
Industry effects	Yes	Yes	Yes
Observations	350	350	350
R-squared	0.288	0.210	0.334

Note: All variables are defined in Appendix A
Standard errors in parentheses. Sig. level: *** $p < 0.01$, ** $p < 0.05$, * $p < 0.1$

The results in column 3 show that the adoption of EMA positively impacts environmental performance at ($\beta = 3.387\ p < 0.01$). This implies that the firm's environmental performance will improve the more EMA is implemented. This finding offers empirical support for the findings of prior studies, such as studies conducted by Erauskin-Tolosa et al. (2020), Gunarathne et al. (2021), Latan et al. (2018) that found a positive relationship between EMA applications and corporate environmental performance. Furthermore, the more advanced the use of EMA improves decision quality and effective organizational control, the more intensified the impact on corporate environmental performance (Chaudhry & Amir, 2020). This result corroborates the stakeholder theory argument and NRBV proposition in which environmental abilities must be developed over time to become valuable and meet stakeholders' expectations (Hart, 1995).

Furthermore, this supports the arguments advanced by Latan et al. (2018) that organizational green resources improve the corporate environmental performance of firms that adopt EMA. In this regard, EMA can constantly improve firms' environmental performance through cost savings regarding resource efficiency and productivity, pollution prevention, and stakeholder relations (Gunarathne et al., 2021). Hypothesis 2 is thus confirmed.

Mediation and Moderation Analysis

According to Hair (2009), the mediation analysis is primarily used to explain the causal chain precisely by defining how or why an independent variable affects the dependent variable. In essence, the role of a mediator variable is to function as a connecting factor between two other variables, one of which is an independent variable and the other of which is a dependent variable. To measure mediating effects, Baron and Kenny (1986) state that certain conditions must be fulfilled for a variable to be deemed a mediator. First, the independent variable (i.e., environmental governance) should significantly affect the dependent variable (i.e., environmental performance). Second, the independent variable (i.e., environmental governance) should significantly affect the mediator variable (i.e., environmental management accounting), as reported in column (2) of Table 4.4. Third, the mediator variable (i.e., environmental management accounting) should significantly affect the dependent variable (i.e., environmental performance). Fourth, if all the above paths are found to be significant, and when introducing the mediator variable (i.e., environmental management accounting), the association between the independent (i.e., environmental governance) and dependent variables (i.e., environmental performance) becomes insignificant, we can conclude that there is evidence of full mediation. However, if the association between the independent and dependent variables remains significant, we can infer that there is evidence of partial mediation.

On the other hand, the moderation analysis demonstrates the link generalizability between the independent and dependent by illustrating the contexts in which the association holds. The moderator variable is a variable that can strengthen, weaken, nullify, or otherwise modulate the link between the independent and dependent variables (Baron & Kenny, 1986). The statistical term "interaction effects" describes moderation effects in business research. The moderator, EMA, interacts with environmental governance in predicting environmental performance and whether the regression weight of environmental performance on environmental governance differs from the EMA function.

Table 4.5 presents the mediation and moderation regression results. The results in column 1 report the mediation analysis. A crucial aspect of this analysis depends on the premise that the direct relationship between the dependent and independent

Table 4.5 Mediation and moderation regression results

Dependent variables →	EP	EP
Independent variables ↓	(4)	(5)
EG	1.518	4.117***
	(0.934)	(0.827)
ENV_MA	2.958***	4.771***
	(0.476)	(0.796)
EMA*EG		3.525***
		(1.186)
BS	0.324	0.268
	(0.596)	(0.589)
CEO_D	−0.272	−0.492
	(1.448)	(1.431)
BI	0.105	0.102*
	(0.074)	(0.573)
BGD	0.080	0.050
	(0.117)	(0.116)
ECS	−0.008	1.014**
	(0.033)	(0.433)
ESI	3.716	5.071
	(3.758)	(3.741)
FS	4.065***	3.820***
	(1.252)	(1.198)
FL	2.215	1.435
	(5.453)	(5.390)
FA	0.013	0.002
	(0.095)	(0.093)
FP	0.037	0.047
	(0.117)	(0.115)
Year effects	Yes	Yes
Firm effects	Yes	Yes
Industry effects	Yes	Yes
Observations	350	350
R-squared	0.378	0.397

Note: All variables are defined in Appendix A
Standard errors in parentheses. Sig. level: *** $p < 0.01$, ** $p < 0.05$, * $p < 0.1$

variables should be significant, as reported in Table 4.4. Nonetheless, when we incorporate EMA as a mediator to the regression, we observe that the previously significant relationship between environmental governance and environmental performance is no longer significant. Overall, this result indicates that EMA fully mediated the relationship between environmental governance and environmental performance. Hypothesis *H3(a)* is thus confirmed.

Column 2 shows the moderating effect of environmental management accounting. To verify hypothesis 3, we introduce the interaction term ($EG \times ENV\_MA$) to examine the moderating effect of EMA on the relationship between environmental governance and environmental performance. The results reveal that the estimated coefficient of the interaction term of the EMA and environmental governance is positive and significant at ($\beta = 3.525$ at $p < 0.01$). This postulated that EMA positively moderates the relationship between environmental governance and environmental performance. Therefore, we find support for hypothesis *H3(b)* relating to the EMA, which strengthens the relationship between environmental governance mechanisms and environmental performance. As for the control variables, the firm size coefficient is positively and significantly associated with corporate environmental performance in all regression models. This result is consistent with prior research indicating that larger firms have more resources and capabilities to handle environmental risk than smaller counterparts (Liao et al., 2015; Moussa et al., 2021).

Overall, our empirical results show that EMA positively and significantly moderates the relationship between environmental governance and corporate environmental performance, which is considered unique to the literature. This makes our findings unique and provides fresh insights into how a firm deals with the effective mechanisms of various green resources, for instance, sustainable board governance and EMA in translating into corporate environmental performance. To the best of our knowledge, this is the first study to apply the moderating impact of EMA between environmental governance and corporate environmental performance, which has not been tested before; consequently, this is a contribution to the existing literature. Further, our results support the hypothesis that the use of EMA fully mediates the relationship between environmental governance and corporate environmental performance. This is a contribution to the existing literature because the mediating role of EMA in environmental governance and corporate environmental performance relationships has not been studied before in this subject. However, the mediating role of EMA and its implications for organizational performance in terms of environmental, economic, and social perspectives have been addressed in many prior studies in the management accounting setting (Asiaei et al., 2021; Gunarathne et al., 2021; Latan et al., 2018).

Extending the literature on environmental management research (e.g., Asiaei et al., 2021; Gunarathne et al., 2021; Latan et al., 2018), we have evidence that EMA and environmental governance matter in enhancing corporate environmental performance. Therefore, we provide further evidence consistent with the theoretical assertions of NRBV and stakeholder theories by indicating the role of EMA and environmental governance in sustaining corporate environmental performance. Building on the resource-based view (RBV), NRBV suggests that the firm strategy and competitive advantage should be built on internal capabilities that enable environmentally friendly economic activities (Hart, 1995). It contends that firms can obtain a competitive advantage by focusing on three strategic capabilities: pollution prevention, product stewardship, and sustainable development policies.

On the other hand, stakeholder theory mainly concerns how organizations manage their business processes with appropriate social and environmental considerations (Friedman, 1984). It depicts that increasing commitment to sustainable environmental practices can improve corporate reputation and image by balancing the conflicts of stakeholder demands (Michelon et al., 2015). Hence, merging all firm sustainability-related strategies, resources, management capabilities, and activities will be relevant antecedents for using EMA, which in turn can improve environmental performance and demonstrate accountability to the stakeholders (Latan et al., 2018). These results highlight the critical role of EMA as an indicator for substantive strategy in examining the relationship between environmental governance and corporate environmental performance. Firms must pay attention to EMA practices to enhance environmental performance and achieve a green image and competitive advantage. Lastly, using the NRBV and stakeholders' lens to see how environmental governance mechanisms affect the environmental performance of the firm through EMA is novel and demonstrates additional application of the theories.

In a nutshell, while corporate environmental performance is reflective of the underlying environmental governance mechanisms, firms have substantive environmental initiatives to demonstrate their environmental stewardship in the presence of robust environmental governance. In contrast, weak environmental governance is predominantly a symbolic approach. These mechanisms are deployed to convey a signal of environmental aspects, but they do not translate into environmental enhancement. This suggests that directors perceive their role through the traditional notion of corporate governance, which concentrates on protecting shareholders' interests and setting aside stakeholders' environmental expectations after managing their perceptions effectively. In addition, the management in firms with weak governance is more inclined to be more involved in discretionary activities. Our empirical findings emphasize that the strong EMA adoption role strains the extent of managerial discretion and greenwashing over their environmental performance by bridging existing gaps between the management and stakeholders and improving the effectiveness of decisions from the board of directors.[4]

Similarly, directors are delineating to prevent litigation, regulatory enforcement costs, and long-term reputational damage. The directors focus on monitoring and tracking financial activities' roles and constrain any potential wrong accounting choices that may affect shareholders' interests. When firms properly classify and allocate environmental costs, they are more likely to demonstrate that the management effectiveness of their resources and capabilities impacts corporate environmental performance. Such an EMA role demonstrates the board's oversight and accountability for climate change challenges and enables it to reach the performance level anticipated by stakeholders. These visions are novel to the literature, postulating the oversight role of the implementation of EMA in enabling awareness and comprehension of the magnitude of physical and monetary environmental information and environmental cost allocation.

[4] Greenwashing can be defined as the gap between the amount of disclosed environmental information and actual corporate environmental performance (Yu et al., 2020).

Robustness Checks

We conduct several robustness checks to increase the reliability of our research. Initially, we ran multicollinearity diagnostics tests. We calculate the value of the variance inflator factors (VIF) and tolerance. For all model variable predictors, the recommended VIF value is 3.3, while 5.0 is still acceptable (Latan et al., 2018). If the VIF value is greater than 10, it is typically interpreted as a sign of multicollinearity or is cause for concern that may be affecting the least-squares estimate (Michelon et al., 2015). As shown in Table 4.3, the highest VIF value is 1.95, providing evidence that there is no multicollinearity problem or cause for concern among predictor variables as it fell within acceptable limits.

Afterward, as an additional analysis, we examine the impact of environmental governance on environmental performance through the role of EMA using alternative measures for the dependent variable. Consistent with prior literature, we employ the greenhouse gas (GHG) emission level of a firm as a proxy for corporate environmental performance (Albitar et al., 2023; Braam et al., 2016; Haque, 2017). The environmental performance is measured as a natural log of total GHG emissions in tons, with higher GHG emissions indicating poor environmental performance. The results are reported in the model (1)–(4) in Table 4.6, illustrating that firms with poorer environmental performance, such as those emitting higher levels of pollutants, are more inclined to engage in EMA practices compared to companies demonstrating superior environmental performance to maintain or reclaim their legitimacy and confer greater confidence among stakeholders. In line with the predictions of our theoretical framework, our findings indicate that results are robust to alternative measures of corporate environmental performance. Collectively, these findings are consistent with those stated in Tables 4.4 and 4.5.

In particular, our findings show that environmental governance is significant and positively associated with environmental performance in terms of GHG emissions (Model 3), suggesting that firms that adopt environmental governance mechanisms seem to be more committed to environmental responsibility and exhibit greater concern for efficiently controlling pollution and mitigating their environmental impact, resulting in a more transparent GHG reporting for the firm. This implies that efforts directed at enhancing corporate environmental performance aimed at reducing the level of GHG emissions should be pursued mutually with those aimed at improving environmental governance practices (Liao et al., 2015). In addition, the coefficient of environmental governance and EMA is still significant in each model. Further, like our earlier analyses, the coefficients of the interaction between environmental governance and EMA remain significant in Model 4. However, a few contrasts are also observed in Table 4.5.

The insignificant coefficient of the interaction between EMA may result from the fact that Italian firms with strong environmental governance ensure the use of appropriate EMA systems to produce good environmental performers in terms of GHG emissions to maintain their legitimacy by managing and reporting their greenhouse gas emissions voluntarily. Interestingly, the coefficient of environmental governance has a positive but weak association, suggesting that EMA fully mediated the

Table 4.6 Alternative measure of environmental performance (GHG_emission)

Dependent variables →	GHG	GHG	GHG (Mediation)	GHG (Moderation)
Dependent variables ↓	(1)	(2)	(3)	(4)
EG	1.567**		1.172*	2.271**
	(0.662)		(0.668)	(1.047)
ENV_MA		1.919***	1.702***	2.809***
		(0.586)	(0.596)	(1.007)
EMA*EG				1.921**
				(0.835)
BS	1.590**	1.507**	1.484**	1.450*
	(0.755)	(0.749)	(0.746)	(0.746)
CEO_D	0.456	0.115	−0.305	−0.439
	(1.816)	(1.803)	(1.812)	(1.812)
BI	0.069	0.081	0.094	0.092
	(0.093)	(0.092)	(0.092)	(0.092)
BGD	0.181	0.114	0.111	0.093
	(0.146)	(0.147)	(0.146)	(0.146)
ECS	−0.020	−0.033	−0.021	−0.025
	(0.042)	(0.042)	(0.042)	(0.042)
ESI	−1.675	1.230	−1.478	−0.651
	(4.766)	(4.461)	(4.704)	(4.736)
FS	9.955**	10.474**	9.152*	9.002*
	(5.377)	(5.289)	(5.322)	(5.315)
FL	6.140	3.979	3.396	2.920
	(6.847)	(6.844)	(6.825)	(6.823)
FA	0.133	0.107	0.093	0.086
	(0.119)	(0.119)	(0.118)	(0.118)
FP	0.834***	0.843***	0.840***	0.846***
	(0.148)	(0.146)	(0.146)	(0.146)
Year effects	Yes	Yes	Yes	Yes
Firm effects	Yes	Yes	Yes	Yes
Industry effects	Yes	Yes	Yes	Yes
Observations	350	350	350	350
R-squared	0.174	0.189	0.199	0.204

Note: All variables are defined in Appendix A
Standard errors in parentheses. Sig. level: *** $p < 0.01$, ** $p < 0.05$, * $p < 0.1$

relationship between environmental governance and environmental performance. In addition, firm performance is no longer statistically significant at conventional levels. However, it was weakly significant in Table 4.4:4.5. Overall, the additional regression results provide us further confidence that we capture the hypothesized effects robustly. These results show that EMA elucidates variances in environmental performance, suggesting that the generation of good corporate environmental performance occurs through the appropriate use of EMA through environmental governance mechanisms. The robustness of environmental governance mechanisms ensures the organization has EMA systems in place, which thereby leads to higher environmental performance. Among the control variables, board size shows a positive relationship. This evidence is consistent with several recent empirical studies that reveal a significant positive influence of board size on environmental disclosures and performance (e.g., Haque & Jones, 2020). Furthermore, firm size largely maintains a positive relationship, indicating that large firms show greater commitment and effectiveness toward reducing environmental emissions in the production and operational processes. Our findings also suggest that leveraged firms are unlikely to prioritize climate-related initiatives due to their short-term operational focus and obligation to pay interest (Haque, 2017).

Chapter 5
Conclusions, Implications, Limitations, and Future Lines of Research

We provide the general conclusions of our study in this chapter, delineating the main contributions of this research to understanding the roles of EMA and governance in enhancing corporate environmental performance information. The implications evaluate the broader significance of these insights for regulators, policymakers, business practitioners, and academic researchers, suggesting practical and policy-oriented applications that align with corporate sustainability goals. The limitations critically reflect the constraints of the study, including methodological and contextual factors, which may influence the applicability and scope of the findings. Finally, the future lines of research identify promising directions for continued analysis. It encourages further exploration of environmental accounting's integration with corporate governance practices and its evolving influence on sustainability reporting outlines and environmental performance. In this respect, this study examines the mediating and moderating role of EMA in the relationship between environmental governance mechanisms and corporate environmental performance. Using a sample of Italian FTSE-listed firms covering the years 2017–2021 period, we found that environmental governance mechanisms significantly affected corporate environmental performance. Specifically, we found that the adoption of GRI guidelines, board sustainability committee, environmental risk horizon, and sustainability assurance positively affects corporate environmental performance. Our findings also revealed that adopting EMA practices positively affected corporate environmental performance. The components of EMA (i.e., environmental management team, emission trading initiatives, environmental expenditures investments, environmentally friendly products, environmental training, sustainability awards, and environmental management system certifications) have a strong, positive, and significant influence on corporate environmental performance. Further, we find that EMA moderates and fully mediates the relationship between environmental governance mechanisms and environmental performance.

M. Aman, L. Lucianetti, *Corporate Environmental Performance and Environmental Management Accounting Systems*, SIDREA Series in Accounting and Business Administration, https://doi.org/10.1007/978-3-031-84947-3_5

The results support insights drawn from the natural resource-based view and stakeholder theories. A natural resource-based perspective contends that environmental protection strategies support the development of distinctive, valuable, and irreplaceable resources that contribute to cleaner production and build legitimacy with society. In this regard, the firm's competitiveness would be boosted through these unique resources by the high demand for its products and services, which would impact its long-term profits and performance. In the same vein, stakeholder theory advocates that the firm's application of environmental management practices enhances its image and reputation and obtains a competitive advantage as acknowledged by the stakeholders, resulting in improved performance. The positive association of EMA practices and environmental performance documented by the study confirmed the natural resource-based view and stakeholder argument that the development of unique resources through efficient implementation of environmental management practices can positively influence environmental performance. More specifically, the study emphasized the role of EMA in supporting the firms to synchronize better, measure, and manage their capabilities, thereby yielding better environmental performance. This result corroborates the firm's view of the NRBV and the relevant three strategies for advancing a firm's current resources and capabilities toward environmental performance. More precisely, EMA will allow top managers to make any environmental decisions more accurately and efficiently, thereby minimizing the waste of resources or inefficient prevention of environmental pollution (Tashakor et al., 2019). Keeping in view NRBV, it emphasizes organizations' ability to address environmental challenges by enhancing their capabilities to efficiently utilize natural resources, thereby establishing a linkage between EMA and environmental performance. In a sense, this evidence induces firms to implement well-aligned EMA practices thoroughly rather than focus only on environmental governance mechanisms to translate firm capabilities into environmental performance.

This study's contributions to EMA mainstream literature and the results offer important implications in theory and practice. Theoretically, it provides valuable insight into the literature as it will narrow the existing gap regarding the boundary between EMA, environmental governance mechanisms, and corporate environmental performance. This study sheds further light on the intervening role of EMA in the decision-making process and control mechanisms that ultimately enhance corporate environmental performance. Practically, this study's conclusions provide a number of implications for regulators, policymakers, and business practitioners. Globally, the net-zero emissions goals for the industrial sector have become a prominent topic in the worldwide media and the press. Italy exemplifies how strict environmental rules imposed on firms can voluntarily implement complete environmental policies as a model for other industrial economies. Therefore, it would be a step in the right direction for other economies to create corporate environmental norms that are most likely to assist in meeting present climate concerns through the long-term vision. This study will be particularly important for strategy makers to realize EMA's importance in developing strategies and policies and improving firms' environmental effectiveness. In particular, policymakers need to develop comprehensive plans to support firms in cultivating and undertaking the necessary environmental protection investment by implementing EMA. Regulatory pressures can also play a critical role in grabbing organizational attention to enable the adoption of sustainable practices and involvement in environmental issues by requiring corporate actions to invest in and use EMA systems. While EMA adoption is costly and has uncertain financial returns, policymakers should assist firms in adopting EMA by providing practical and financial support. Thus, they have to provide more detailed guidelines about EMA implementation and how many benefits can be obtained. Despite the potential reluctance of policymakers and firms to increase expenditure due to unprecedented economic post-COVID and geopolitical challenges, such green investments are vital for global economic growth and align with the 2021 United Nations Climate Change Conference (COP26) goals for reducing global warming (Guérin & Suntheim, 2021). Moreover, the findings will assist firms in understanding the role of legislation, regulations, norms, standards, and competition actions in driving EMA adoption and environmental performance improvements.

Empirical findings from the environmental management literature highlight the importance of EMA in environmental reporting processes, supporting a drive toward a more plausible accounting system as advocated by Jones (2010). These results thus help firms report environmental performance and build and maintain relationships with stakeholders as driving forces in environmentally responsive decision-making. This also offers insights for policymakers conducting environmental audits of the whole environmental management system on firm performance.

This study has some limitations that promise avenues for future research. Firstly, we conducted this analysis focusing on Italian non-financial firms (NF) as financial firms, including banks, were not considered for the analysis. In addition, this study examines 70 non-financial firms from the more capitalized Italian Stock Exchange index, the FTSE, providing results for large listed firms. Then, it poses the generalizations issue. Future studies should explore the role of EMA between environmental governance and performance in other economic and cultural regulatory environments. For instance, future research could, therefore, enlarge the sample to listed and not-listed firms, including medium and small-sized and family business firms. In addition, future research can also extend this empirical analysis to consider different countries by conducting a cross-country study to generate more generalizable results. Secondly, the study covers the period after implementing Legislative Decree 254/2016. Considering that environmental governance mechanisms, EMA, and environmental performance are constantly in a state of flux, future studies can consider the period before applying the Italian law to compare the evolutionary nature that impacts environmental performance before and after the decree was enforced. Equally, research data from 2022 and 2023 may also show the impact of the unexpected COVID-19 pandemic outbreaks, which have tremendously affected the world economy and health. In particular, researchers can add further insights by conducting longitudinal studies that consider the environmental concerns' outcomes; such effects can only be observed in the long term. Thirdly, this study aimed to investigate the role of EMA in general and across various industries. Our findings, however, are limited in their ability to provide decision-makers with information in specific environmental domains, whether in terms of physical or monetary terms, like energy, water, materials, carbon, waste, and biodiversity on the most influential environmental management strategies for each of these distinct contexts. Therefore, future research should consider these contexts of a particular sector while assessing the effect of environmental governance on performance, considering EMA practices' role within that industry.

Appendix A Description and Measurement of Variables

No.	Variables	Notations	Definitions
Main variables			
1	Environmental performance	EP	Environmental performance data was extracted based on Thomson Reuter's ratings
2	Environmental governance	EG	Environmental governance strength is calculated as the collective score of the 4 variable components
3	GRI guidelines	GRI	Coded "1" if the firm publishes a CSR or sustainability report in accordance with GRI guidelines for each year, "0" otherwise
4	Board sustainability committee	B_SC	Coded "1" if the firm has a sustainability committee, "0" otherwise
5	Corporate emission reduction target	CERT	If the emission reduction target is set as far as less than 3 years—4 points; 4–7 years—3 points; over 7 years—2 points; unidentified—1 point; none—0 points
6	Sustainability assurance	SA	Coded "1" if the firm has an external auditor of its sustainability report, 0 points otherwise.
7	Environmental management accounting	ENV_MA	Environmental management accounting data is calculated as the collective score of the 7 variable components
8	Environmental management team	EM_Team	Coded "1" if the firm has a dedicated management team responsible for environmental issues and coordinating accounting, environmental management, and operational data, "0" otherwise
9	Emissions trading	ET	Coded "1" if the firm reports on its participation in any emissions trading initiative, "0" otherwise
10	Environmental expenditures investments	EEI	Coded "1" if the firm reports to make proactive environmental investments to reduce future risks or increase future opportunities, "0" otherwise

(continued)

M. Aman, L. Lucianetti, *Corporate Environmental Performance and Environmental Management Accounting Systems*, SIDREA Series in Accounting and Business Administration, https://doi.org/10.1007/978-3-031-84947-3

No.	Variables	Notations	Definitions
11	Environmental products	EP	Coded "1" if the firm reports at least one product line or service that is designed to have positive effects on the environment, "0" otherwise
12	Environment management training	EMT	Coded "1" if the firm conducts training for employees on environmental issues, "0" otherwise
13	Sustainability awards	CSRAW	Coded "1" if the firm received awards for its socio-environmental performance, "0" otherwise
14	Environmental management system	CERTIFICATE	Coded "1" if the firm holds an environmental management system (EMS) or environmental certificate (ISO14001), "0" otherwise
Control variables			
15	Board size	BS	Total number of directors on board
16	Board independence	BI	Percentage of independent directors on board
17	Executive duality	CEO_D	Same person CEO and chairman = "1", otherwise = "0"
18	Board gender diversity	B_GD	Percentage of women's representation on boards.
19	Environmentally sensitive industry	ESI	Coded "1" if the firm operates in environmentally sensitive industries, "0" otherwise
20	Environmentally controversies sensitivity	ECS	The firm exposure score to environmental controversy and adverse events is reflected in global media.
21	Firm size	FS	Natural logarithm of total assets
22	Firm age	FA	Log years by firm's establishment
23	Firm leverage	FL	Long-term liabilities divided by total assets
24	Financial performance	FP	EBIT divided by total assets

References

Albitar, K., Al-Shaer, H., & Liu, Y. S. (2023). Corporate commitment to climate change: The effect of eco-innovation and climate governance. *Research Policy, 52*(2), 104697.

Angerio, V. D. (2020). Clima, BlackRock compila la lista nera delle società e boccia 244 colossi. *Il Sole 24 ORE*, 1–2. https://www.ilsole24ore.com/art/clima-blackrock-compila-lista-nera-bocciati-244-colossi-ADjW39d

Appannan, J. S., Mohd Said, R., Ong, T. S., & Senik, R. (2023). Promoting sustainable development through strategies, environmental management accounting and environmental performance. *Business Strategy and the Environment, 32*(4), 1914–1930.

Asiaei, K., Bontis, N., Alizadeh, R., & Yaghoubi, M. (2021). *Green intellectual capital and environmental management accounting: Natural resource orchestration in favor of environmental performance* (pp. 1–18). Business Strategy and the Environment. https://doi.org/10.1002/bse.2875

Asiaei, K., O'Connor, N. G., Barani, O., & Joshi, M. (2023). Green intellectual capital and ambidextrous green innovation: The impact on environmental performance. *Business Strategy and the Environment, 32*(1), 369–386.

Asiri, N., Khan, T., & Kend, M. (2020). Environmental management accounting in the Middle East and North Africa region: Significance of resource slack and coercive isomorphism. *Journal of Cleaner Production, 267*, 121870.

Baron, R. M., & Kenny, D. A. (1986). The moderator-mediator variable distinction in social psychological research: Conceptual, strategic, and statistical considerations. *Journal of Personality and Social Psychology, 51*(6), 1173–1182. https://doi.org/10.1037/0022-3514.51.6.1173

Bartolomeo, M., Bennett, M., Bouma, J. J., Heydkamp, P., James, P., & Wolters, T. (2000). Environmental management accounting in Europe: Current practice and future potential. *European Accounting Review, 9*(1), 31–52.

Berrone, P., & Gomez-Mejia, L. R. (2009). Environmental performance and executive compensation: An integrated agency-institutional perspective. *Academy of Management Journal, 52*(1), 103–126.

Berrone, P., Cruz, C., Gomez-Mejia, L. R., & Larraza-Kintana, M. (2010). Socioemotional wealth and corporate responses to institutional pressures: Do family-controlled firms pollute less? *Administrative Science Quarterly, 55*(1), 82–113. https://doi.org/10.2189/asqu.2010.55.1.82

Blundell, R., & Bond, S. (1998). Initial conditions and moment restrictions in dynamic panel data models. *Journal of Econometrics, 87*(1), 115–143.

Boakye, D. J., Tingbani, I., Ahinful, G. S., & Nsor-Ambala, R. (2021). The relationship between environmental management performance and financial performance of firms listed in the

M. Aman, L. Lucianetti, *Corporate Environmental Performance and Environmental Management Accounting Systems*, SIDREA Series in Accounting and Business Administration, https://doi.org/10.1007/978-3-031-84947-3

alternative investment market (AIM) in the UK. *Journal of Cleaner Production, 278*, 124034. https://doi.org/10.1016/j.jclepro.2020.124034

Braam, G. J. M., de Weerd, L. U., Hauck, M., & Huijbregts, M. A. J. (2016). Determinants of corporate environmental reporting: The importance of environmental performance and assurance. *Journal of Cleaner Production, 129*, 724–734.

Brooks, C., & Oikonomou, I. (2018). The effects of environmental, social and governance disclosures and performance on firm value: A review of the literature in accounting and finance. *The British Accounting Review, 50*(1), 1–15.

Bui, B., Houqe, M. N., & Zaman, M. (2020). Climate governance effects on carbon disclosure and performance. *British Accounting Review, 52*(2), 100880. https://doi.org/10.1016/j.bar.2019.100880

Buntaine, M. T. (2011). Does the Asian Development Bank respond to past environmental performance when allocating environmentally risky financing? *World Development, 39*(3), 336–350.

Burritt, R. L., Hahn, T., & Schaltegger, S. (2002). Towards a comprehensive framework for environmental management accounting—Links between business actors and environmental management accounting tools. *Australian Accounting Review, 12*(27), 39–50.

Burritt, R. L., Herzig, C., Schaltegger, S., & Viere, T. (2019). Diffusion of environmental management accounting for cleaner production: Evidence from some case studies. *Journal of Cleaner Production, 224*, 479–491.

Carlsson-Wall, M., Kraus, K., & Messner, M. (2016). Performance measurement systems and the enactment of different institutional logics: Insights from a football organization. *Management Accounting Research, 32*, 45–61.

Chaudhry, N. I., & Amir, M. (2020). From institutional pressure to the sustainable development of firm: Role of environmental management accounting implementation and environmental proactivity. *Business Strategy and the Environment, 29*(8), 3542–3554.

Chen, S., Song, Y., & Gao, P. (2023). Environmental, social, and governance (ESG) performance and financial outcomes: Analyzing the impact of ESG on financial performance. *Journal of Environmental Management, 345*, 118829.

Cho, C. H., Roberts, R. W., & Patten, D. M. (2010). The language of US corporate environmental disclosure. *Accounting, Organizations and Society, 35*(4), 431–443.

Christ, K. L., & Burritt, R. L. (2013). Environmental management accounting: The significance of contingent variables for adoption. *Journal of Cleaner Production, 41*, 163–173. https://doi.org/10.1016/j.jclepro.2012.10.007

Clarkson, P. M., Li, Y., Richardson, G. D., & Vasvari, F. P. (2008). Revisiting the relation between environmental performance and environmental disclosure: An empirical analysis. *Accounting, Organizations and Society, 33*(4–5), 303–327.

Clementino, E., & Perkins, R. (2021). How do companies respond to environmental, social and governance (ESG) ratings? Evidence from Italy. *Journal of Business Ethics, 171*(2), 379–397. https://doi.org/10.1007/s10551-020-04441-4

Combs, J. G., Crook, T. R., & Shook, C. L. (2005). The dimensionality of organizational performance and its implications for strategic management research. In *Research methodology in strategy and management*. Emerald Group Publishing Limited.

De Villiers, C., & Van Staden, C. J. (2011). Where firms choose to disclose voluntary environmental information. *Journal of Accounting and Public Policy, 30*(6), 504–525.

de Villiers, C., Naiker, V., & Van Staden, C. J. (2011). The effect of board characteristics on firm environmental performance. *Journal of Management, 37*(6), 1636–1663.

de Villiers, C., Jia, J., & Li, Z. (2022). Are boards' risk management committees associated with firms' environmental performance? *The British Accounting Review, 54*(1), 101066.

Deegan, C. (2017). Critical Perspectives on Accounting Twenty fi ve years of social and environmental accounting research within Critical Perspectives of Accounting: Hits, misses and ways forward. *Critical Perspectives on Accounting, 43*, 65–87. https://doi.org/10.1016/j.cpa.2016.06.005

Ding, X., Ye, L., Yang, Y., Efimova, O., Steblyanskaya, A., & Zhang, J. (2022). The impact mechanism of environmental information disclosure on corporate sustainability performance—micro-evidence from China. *Sustainability, 14*(19), 12366.

Dragomir, V. D. (2018). How do we measure corporate environmental performance? A critical review. *Journal of Cleaner Production, 196*, 1124–1157. https://doi.org/10.1016/j.jclepro.2018.06.014

Drury, C. M. (2013). *Management and cost accounting*. Springer.

Dutta, S. K., Lawson, R. A., & Marcinko, D. J. (2013). Alignment of performance measurement to sustainability objectives: A variance-based framework. *Journal of Accounting and Public Policy, 32*(6), 456–474.

Environmental Protection Agency (EPA). (1995). *An introduction to environmental accounting as a business management tool: key concepts and terms*. US Environmental Protection Agency, Office of Pollution Prevention and Toxics.

Erauskin-Tolosa, A., Zubeltzu-Jaka, E., Heras-Saizarbitoria, I., & Boiral, O. (2020). ISO 14001, EMAS and environmental performance: A meta-analysis. *Business Strategy and the Environment, 29*(3), 1145–1159. https://doi.org/10.1002/bse.2422

Ferreira, A., Moulang, C., & Hendro, B. (2010). Environmental management accounting and innovation : an exploratory analysis. *Accounting, Auditing & Accountability Journal, 23*(7), 920–948. https://doi.org/10.1108/09513571011080180

Fisher, D. R., Jasny, L., Redmond, J., & Heaume, F. (2021). Environmental governance. *Handbooks of Sociology and Social Research, 31*(1), 333–353. https://doi.org/10.1007/978-3-030-77712-8_16

Franco-santos, M., Lucianetti, L., & Bourne, M. (2012). Contemporary performance measurement systems: A review of their consequences and a framework for research. *Management Accounting Research, 23*(2), 79–119. https://doi.org/10.1016/j.mar.2012.04.001

Friedman, R. (1984). *Strategic management: A stakeholder perspective*. Prentice-Hall.

Gerged, A. M., Zahoor, N., & Cowton, C. J. (2024). Understanding the relationship between environmental management accounting and firm performance: The role of environmental innovation and stakeholder integration–evidence from a developing country. *Management Accounting Research, 62*, 100865.

Ghosh, R., & Wolf, S. (2021). Hybrid governance and performances of environmental accounting. *Journal of Environmental Management, 284*, 111995.

Gibassier, D., & Schaltegger, S. (2015). Carbon management accounting and reporting in practice: A case study on converging emergent approaches. *Sustainability Accounting, Management and Policy Journal, 6*(3), 340–365.

Gilley, K. M., Worrell, D. L., Davidson, W. N., III, & El-Jelly, A. (2000). Corporate environmental initiatives and anticipated firm performance: The differential effects of process-driven versus product-driven greening initiatives. *Journal of Management, 26*(6), 1199–1216.

Gomez-Conde, J., Lunkes, R. J., & Rosa, F. S. (2019). Environmental innovation practices and operational performance. The joint effects of management accounting and control systems and environmental training. *Accounting, Auditing and Accountability Journal*.

GRI, G. R. I. (2002). *Sustainability reporting guidelines*. GRI: Boston, MA.

Guérin, P., & Suntheim, F. (2021). Firms' environmental performance and the COVID-19 crisis. *Economics Letters, 205*, 109956. https://doi.org/10.1016/j.econlet.2021.109956

Gunarathne, N., & Lee, K.-H. (2015). Environmental management accounting (EMA) for environmental management and organizational change. *Journal of Accounting & Organizational Change, 11*(3), 362–383. https://doi.org/10.1108/JAOC-10-2013-0078

Gunarathne, N., & Lee, K. (2021). Corporate cleaner production strategy development and environmental management accounting: A contingency theory perspective. *Journal of Cleaner Production, 308*(December 2020), 127402.

Gunarathne, A. D. N., Lee, K. H., & Hitigala Kaluarachchilage, P. K. (2021). Institutional pressures, environmental management strategy, and organizational performance: The role of environmental management accounting. *Business Strategy and the Environment, 30*(2), 825–839. https://doi.org/10.1002/bse.2656

Gunarathne, N., Lee, K.-H., & Hitigala Kaluarachchilage, P. K. (2023). Tackling the integration challenge between environmental strategy and environmental management accounting. *Accounting, Auditing & Accountability Journal, 36*(1), 63–95.

Günther, E., & Kaulich, S. (2005). The EPM-KOMPAS: An instrument to control the environmental performance in small and medium-sized enterprises (SMEs). *Business Strategy and the Environment, 14*(6), 361–371.

Guo, M., Kuai, Y., & Liu, X. (2020). Stock market response to environmental policies: Evidence from heavily polluting firms in China. *Economic Modelling, 86*(71401141), 306–316. https://doi.org/10.1016/j.econmod.2019.09.028

Hair, J. F. (2009). *Multivariate data analysis*.

Hanif, S., Ahmed, A., & Younas, N. (2023). Examining the impact of environmental management accounting practices and green transformational leadership on corporate environmental performance: The mediating role of green process innovation. *Journal of Cleaner Production, 414*, 137584.

Haque, F. (2017). The effects of board characteristics and sustainable compensation policy on carbon performance of UK firms. *The British Accounting Review, 49*(3), 347–364.

Haque, F., & Jones, M. J. (2020). European firms' corporate biodiversity disclosures and board gender diversity from 2002 to 2016. *British Accounting Review, 52*(2), 100893. https://doi.org/10.1016/j.bar.2020.100893

Hart, S. L. (1995). A natural-resource-based view of the firm. *Academy of Management Review, 20*(4), 986–1014.

Hartmann, J., & Vachon, S. (2018). Linking environmental management to environmental performance: The interactive role of industry context. *Business Strategy and the Environment, 27*(3), 359–374. https://doi.org/10.1002/bse.2003

Henri, J., & Journeault, M. (2010). Eco-control: The influence of management control systems on environmental and economic performance. *Accounting, Organizations and Society, 35*(1), 63–80.

Hillman, A. J., & Dalziel, T. (2003). Boards of directors and firm performance: Integrating agency and resource dependence perspectives. *Academy of Management Review, 28*(3), 383–396.

IFAC. (2005). *International guidance document on environmental management accounting*. IFAC.

Ilinitch, A. Y., Soderstrom, N. S., & Thomas, T. E. (1998). Measuring corporate environmental performance. *Journal of Accounting and Public Policy, 17*(4–5), 383–408.

ISO. (2013). *International Organization for Standardization (ISO). ISO 14031:2013. Environmental management —Environmental performance evaluation —Guidelines*. Available at https://www.iso.org/obp/ui/#iso:std:iso:14031:ed-2:v1:en

Johnstone, L. (2020). The construction of environmental performance in ISO 14001-certified SMEs. *Journal of Cleaner Production, 263*, 121559.

Jones, M. J. (2010). Accounting for the environment: Towards a theoretical perspective for environmental accounting and reporting. *Accounting Forum, 34*(2), 123–138.

Journeault, M., De Ronge, Y., & Henri, J.-F. (2016). Levers of eco-control and competitive environmental strategy. *The British Accounting Review, 48*(3), 316–340.

Judge, W. Q., & Douglas, T. J. (1998). Performance implications of incorporating natural environmental issues into the strategic planning process: An empirical assessment. *Journal of Management Studies, 35*(2), 241–262.

Kang, A., Ren, L., Hua, C., Song, H., Dong, M., Fang, Z., & Zhu, M. (2021). Environmental management strategy in response to COVID-19 in China: Based on text mining of government open information. *Science of the Total Environment, 769*, 145158.

Latan, H., Diponegoro, U., & Issues, M. (2018). Linking environmental strategy to environmental performance : Mediation role of environmental management accounting sustainability accounting. *Management and Policy Journal, 8*, 595. https://doi.org/10.1108/SAMPJ-08-2016-0046

Law, K. S., Wong, C.-S., & Mobley, W. M. (1998). Toward a taxonomy of multidimensional constructs. *Academy of Management Review, 23*(4), 741–755.

Li, W., Zheng, M., Zhang, Y., & Cui, G. (2020). Green governance structure, ownership characteristics, and corporate financing constraints. *Journal of Cleaner Production*, 121008.

Liao, L., Luo, L., & Tang, Q. (2015). Gender diversity, board independence, environmental committee and greenhouse gas disclosure. *The British Accounting Review, 47*(4), 409–424.

Lisi, I. E. (2015). Translating environmental motivations into performance: The role of environmental performance measurement systems. *Management Accounting Research, 29*, 27–44.

Maas, K., Schaltegger, S., & Crutzen, N. (2016). Advancing the integration of corporate sustainability measurement, management and reporting. *Journal of Cleaner Production, 133*, 859–862. https://doi.org/10.1016/j.jclepro.2016.06.006

Marrucci, L., Daddi, T., & Iraldo, F. (2022). Do dynamic capabilities matter? A study on environmental performance and the circular economy in European certified organisations. *Business Strategy and the Environment, 31*(6), 2641–2657.

Michelon, G., Pilonato, S., & Ricceri, F. (2015). CSR reporting practices and the quality of disclosure: An empirical analysis. *Critical Perspectives on Accounting, 33*, 59–78.

Michelon, G., Rodrigue, M., & Trevisan, E. (2020). The marketization of a social movement: Activists, shareholders and CSR disclosure. *Accounting, Organizations and Society, 80*, 101074. https://doi.org/10.1016/j.aos.2019.101074

Mokhtar, N., Jusoh, R., & Zulkifli, N. (2016). Corporate characteristics and environmental management accounting (EMA) implementation: evidence from Malaysian public listed companies (PLCs). *Journal of Cleaner Production, 136*, 111–122. https://doi.org/10.1016/j.jclepro.2016.01.085

Morioka, S. N., & Carvalho, M. M. (2016). Measuring sustainability in practice: exploring the inclusion of sustainability into corporate performance systems in Brazilian case studies. *Journal of Cleaner Production, 136*, 123–133.

Moussa, T., Kotb, A., & Helfaya, A. (2021). An empirical investigation of U.K. environmental targets disclosure: The role of environmental governance and performance. *European Accounting Review, 0*(0), 1–35.

Muhammad, H., & Migliori, S. (2023). Effects of board gender diversity and sustainability committees on environmental performance: A quantile regression approach. *Journal of Management & Organization, 29*(6), 1051–1076.

Muhammad, H., Migliori, S., & Mohsni, S. (2022). Corporate governance and R&D investment: The role of debt financing. *Industrial and Corporate Change, 31*(3), 628–653. https://doi.org/10.1093/icc/dtab056

Mungai, E. M., Ndiritu, S. W., & Rajwani, T. (2020). Do voluntary environmental management systems improve environmental performance? Evidence from waste management by Kenyan firms. *Journal of Cleaner Production, 265*, 121636.

Naranjo Tuesta, Y., Crespo Soler, C., & Ripoll Feliu, V. (2021). Carbon management accounting and financial performance: Evidence from the European Union emission trading system. *Business Strategy and the Environment, 30*(2), 1270–1282. https://doi.org/10.1002/bse.2683

Neely, A., Gregory, M., & Platts, K. (1995). Performance measurement system design: A literature review and research agenda. *International Journal of Operations & Production Management, 15*(4), 80–116.

Nkundabanyanga, S. K., & Muramuzi, B. (2021). *Environmental management accounting, board role performance, company characteristics and environmental performance disclosure*. https://doi.org/10.1108/JAOC-03-2020-0035

Ntim, C. G., & Soobaroyen, T. (2013). Corporate governance and performance in socially responsible corporations: New empirical insights from a neo-institutional framework. *Corporate Governance: An International Review, 21*(5), 468–494.

Orazalin, N. (2020). Do board sustainability committees contribute to corporate environmental and social performance? The mediating role of corporate social responsibility strategy. *Business Strategy and the Environment., 29*, 140.

Perego, P., & Hartmann, F. (2009). Aligning performance measurement systems with strategy: The case of environmental strategy. *Abacus, 45*(4), 397–428.

Pham, H., Sutton, B. G., Brown, P. J., & Brown, D. A. (2020). Moving towards sustainability: A theoretical design of environmental performance measurement systems. *Journal of Cleaner Production, 269*, 122273. https://doi.org/10.1016/j.jclepro.2020.122273

Pondeville, S., Swaen, V., & Rongé, Y. De. (2013). Environmental management control systems: The role of contextual and strategic factors. *Management Accounting Research, 24*(4), 317–332. https://doi.org/10.1016/j.mar.2013.06.007

Porter, M. E. (2001). The value chain and competitive advantage. *Understanding Business Processes, 2*, 50–66.

Preacher, K. J., & Hayes, A. F. (2008). Asymptotic and resampling strategies for assessing and comparing indirect effects in multiple mediator models. *Behavior Research Methods, 40*(3), 879–891. https://doi.org/10.3758/BRM.40.3.879

Qian, W., Hörisch, J., & Schaltegger, S. (2018). Environmental management accounting and its effects on carbon management and disclosure quality. *Journal of Cleaner Production, 174*, 1608–1619.

Qiu, Y., Shaukat, A., & Tharyan, R. (2016). Environmental and social disclosures: Link with corporate financial performance. *British Accounting Review, 48*(1), 102–116. https://doi.org/10.1016/j.bar.2014.10.007

Rodrigue, M., Magnan, M., & Boulianne, E. (2013). Stakeholders' influence on environmental strategy and performance indicators: A managerial perspective. *Management accounting research, 24*(4), 301–316.

Sands, J., & Lee, K.-H. (2015). Environmental and sustainability management accounting (EMA) for the development of sustainability management and accountability [Guest editorial]. *Issues in Social and Environmental Accounting, 9*(1), 1–4.

Schaltegger, S., Müller, K., & Hindrichsen, H. (1996). *Corporate environmental accounting*. Wiley.

Sharma, S., & Vredenburg, H. (1998). Proactive corporate environmental strategy and the development of competitively valuable organizational capabilities. *Strategic Management Journal, 19*(8), 729–753.

Shen, J., & Chen, Y. (2021). Environmental information disclosure and financial performance - empirical evidence from heavily polluting Industries in China. *E3S Web of Conferences, 261*(5), 2313–2331. https://doi.org/10.1051/e3sconf/202126104038

Solomon, J. (2020). *Corporate governance and accountability*. Wiley.

Tashakor, S., Appuhami, R., & Munir, R. (2019). Environmental management accounting practices in Australian cotton farming. *Accounting, Auditing & Accountability Journal., 32*, 1175. https://doi.org/10.1108/aaaj-04-2018-3465

Trumpp, C., Endrikat, J., Zopf, C., & Guenther, E. (2015). Definition, conceptualization, and measurement of corporate environmental performance: A critical examination of a multidimensional construct. *Journal of Business Ethics, 126*(2), 185–204.

Tsui, C. S. K. (2014). A Literature Review on Environmental Management Accounting (EMA) Adoption, 1(3).

UNDSD (United Nations division for sustainable development). (2001). *Environmental Management Accounting: Procedures and Principles*.

Velte, P. (2023). Determinants and financial consequences of environmental performance and reporting: A literature review of European archival research. *Journal of Environmental Management, 340*, 117916.

Veltri, S., & Ferraro, O. (2018). Does other comprehensive income matter in credit-oriented systems? Analyzing the Italian context. *Journal of International Accounting, Auditing and Taxation, 30*, 18–31.

Wang, S., Wang, H., & Wang, J. (2018). Exploring the effects of institutional pressures on the implementation of environmental management accounting: Do top management support and perceived benefit work? *Business Strategy and the Environment, 28*(1), 233–243. https://doi.org/10.1002/bse.2252

WEF. (2019). *How to set up effective climate governance on corporate boards. Guiding principles and questions*. In collaboration with PwC. World Economic Forum. http://www3.weforum.org/docs/WEF_Creating_effective_climate_governance_on_corporate_boards.pdf

Yu, L., Van, B., & Chen, C. H. (2020). Greenwashing in environmental, social and governance disclosures. *Research in International Business and Finance, 52*, 101192. https://doi.org/10.1016/j.ribaf.2020.101192

Zhang, D., & Wellalage, N. H. (2022). Comparative analysis of environmental performance measures and their impact on firms' financing choices. *Journal of Cleaner Production, 375*, 134–176.

Zeiler, L. J. (2004). Boards of directors as an endogenously determined institution: A survey of the economic literature. *CFA Digest, 34*(1), 21–22. https://doi.org/10.2469/dig.v34.n1.1410

Zhu, X., He, M., & Li, H. (2021). Environmental regulation, governance transformation and the green development of Chinese iron and steel enterprises. *Journal of Cleaner Production, 328, 129557*.

MIX
Papier aus verantwortungsvollen Quellen
Paper from responsible sources
FSC® C105338

If you have any concerns about our products,
you can contact us on
ProductSafety@springernature.com

In case Publisher is established outside the EU,
the EU authorized representative is:
Springer Nature Customer Service Center GmbH
Europaplatz 3, 69115 Heidelberg, Germany

Printed by Libri Plureos GmbH
in Hamburg, Germany